# GLIMPSES OF AN INVISIBLE GOD

## FOR TEACHERS

Experiencing God in the
Everyday Moments of Life

RACINE, WI

*Glimpses of an Invisible God - for Teachers*
ISBN: 979-8-88898-027-9 - *Paperback*
ISBN: 979-8-88898-028-6 - *Hardcover*
ISBN: 979-8-88898-029-3 - *Ebook*
Copyright © 2023 by Honor Books
Racine, WI

Cover design by Faille Schmitz.
Manuscript written by Vicki Kuyper and Stephen Parolini.

# INTRODUCTION

More than ever before, teachers are searching— longing for a deeper relationship with God. Most have no problem recognizing His distinguished hand in the bright hues of the rainbow, the magnificent grandeur of the night sky, or the breathtaking vistas of the Grand Canyon. But many hope for more. *Is He present in the classroom and routine moments of my everyday life?* they wonder.

If you have been asking that question, *Glimpses of an Invisible God for Teachers* is written specifically for you. As you move through its pages, you will visit the everyday existence of educators like yourself, and you will have an opportunity to learn how they experience God in both the great and small details of their lives.

We trust you will be blessed as you discover the depth of God's love for you and His commitment to walk with you down the halls of your school and the avenues of your life.

*He who began a good work in you will carry it on to completion.*

**PHILIPPIANS 1:6 NIV**

---

*So if you find life difficult because you're doing what God said, take it in stride. Trust him. He knows what he's doing, and he'll keep on doing it.*

**1 PETER 4:19 MSG**

---

*Commit your work to the Lord, then it will succeed.*

**PROVERBS 16:3 TLB**

# UNTO GOD

The Christmas play was coming along beautifully — or at least the principal had said so; yet the choir teacher, Melissa, couldn't get her fingers to cooperate. Although she had accompanied the high school vocalist each year, she suddenly couldn't hit the right keys on the piano. Am I distracted? she thought. She continued to pound out the notes, but her joy was gone and concerned looks crossed her students' faces.

After twenty minutes without success, Melissa rushed off the platform and ran backstage. Pam, a concerned parent and friend, followed her. "Melissa, I know you have a lot going on. Maybe you're trying too hard."

"No, that's not it," Melissa sobbed, "I have too much to do and I can't focus. I have no time to practice, no time to think."

"Melissa, God has given you a gift, and He promised to complete the work that He started in you. Go home and get alone with Him. Do what He impresses you to do. He is faithful to complete His work. All you have to do is trust Him."

The next week Pam saw Melissa walking across the school parking lot before rehearsal. Melissa looked relaxed and refreshed. The stress and worry were gone.

"I found time with the Lord and time for practice. My playing changed when I played for God and not for others. I'm ready," Melissa called to Pam with a smile.

> **WHEN GOD COMES FIRST, EVERYTHING ELSE TAKES ITS PLACE.**

*"Man looks at the outward appearance, but the Lord looks at the heart."*

**1 SAMUEL 16:7 NKJV**

———————

*You made my whole being; you formed me in my mother's body.*

**PSALM 139:13 NCV**

———————

*Humans are satisfied with whatever looks good; God probes for what is good.*

**PROVERBS 16:2 MSG**

# HE'S LOOKING AT YOU

English literature teacher Jeremy stood in front of his desk daily amid student criticisms of his large frame. Coming home, he dropped his new gym bag on the ottoman and flopped down, exhausted, in front of the television. The worn cushions of the couch welcomed him, giving way under his weight. He clicked on the television.

"And in only thirty days, you can have a body like this too." Perfectly toned bodies effortlessly demonstrated some "ab relocator 3000" device. Jeremy stared across the room into the mirror, sighed, and pushed the off button. Just then the phone rang. It was Lynn. "Jeremy, I just wanted to tell you how much I appreciate what you did. You have such a good heart. God must smile when He looks at you."

"God must smile . . ." The words echoed loudly inside Jeremy's heart all evening. A smile—from God? Jeremy took a moment to thank God for helping him see himself in a whole new way—God's way.

Have you ever seen yourself as God sees you?

---

**DON'T ASK THE MIRROR, "HOW DO I LOOK?" ASK GOD.**

*According to his promise we wait for
new heavens and a new earth in which
righteousness dwells.*

## 2 PETER 3:13 RSV

*We are citizens of heaven, where the
Lord Jesus Christ lives. And we are
eagerly waiting for him to return as
our Savior.*

## PHILIPPIANS 3:20 NLT

*Whoever believes in Him should not
perish but have eternal life.*

## JOHN 3:15 NKJV

# CAN HARDLY WAIT

The first-graders were more restless than usual. *Is it the snowstorm?* Lucy wondered. *No, maybe they're just being first-graders*, she reasoned, then laughed at her simple conclusion. "What's so funny, Ms. Hawkins?" Jennie asked, looking up at her with the biggest green eyes Lucy had ever seen on a seven-year-old.

"Just daydreaming," she replied. Then she got an idea. "Class, we're going to do something a little different. We're going to tell about our dreams and hopes." Alec went first. He wanted to be a basketball player. So did Brent. And Nathan. And Michael. And even Monica. But then Jennie stood up to share.

"I dream about what Heaven's like—what kinds of food they have there, if I can jump really, really high! My mom says that's where my grandpa lives, and Jesus lives there too." For a moment, no one spoke. Then everyone started talking at once. As she listened to the children, Lucy caught some of the excitement herself. Her students had bigger dreams than she had imagined.

> TO BELIEVE IN HEAVEN IS NOT TO RUN AWAY FROM LIFE; IT IS TO RUN TOWARD IT.

*Pour out your heart like water in the presence of the Lord.*

**LAMENTATIONS 2:19**

---

*Cast thy burden upon the Lord, and he shall sustain thee.*

**PSALM 55:22 KJV**

---

*When the righteous cry for help, the Lord hears, and delivers them out of all their troubles.*

**PSALM 34:17 RSV**

# HERE COMES THE FLOOD

Susan spent a frustrating and tearful hour on the phone with her mother. Then her son's teacher called to tell her Sean was failing geometry. Her husband, Gary, left a message that he was looking at another all-nighter at the office. The dog got into the pantry again while she spent the afternoon substitute teaching in her daughter's classroom. She was ready to explode.

It was time to find a quiet place where she could open the floodgates and let God know how she was feeling. She knew that God didn't mind it when she cried and even yelled. He could handle her frustration, so she let it all go!

When she had said all she had to say, Susan took a little more time—a few God moments—to let Him fill her with good things like peace, patience, love, and wisdom.

Are there some things you need to talk to God about? Be honest—He can take it. And telling Him will help you make it!

GOD TAKES LIFE'S PIECES AND GIVES US UNBROKEN PEACE.

*Some trust in chariots and some in horses, but we trust in the name of the Lord our God.*

**PSALM 20:7**

---

*Those who know your name trust in you, for you, O Lord, have never abandoned anyone who searches for you.*

**PSALM 9:10 NLT**

---

*The ways of God are without fault; the Lord's words are pure. He is a shield to those who trust him.*

**2 SAMUEL 22:31 NCV**

# IN GOD WE TRUST

Gretchen ran her life like a finely tuned machine. She could be reached any time of the day or night by phone, fax, e-mail, or cell. Her diet was nutritionally balanced. Her social calendar was full, and most of the time her classroom ran like clockwork with her firm hand of control. With the help of her personal trainer, financial advisor, and fashion consultant, she felt she had her life well under control. That is, until the accident.

Gretchen's life was changed in a moment. But there in her hospital bed, she remembered her mother's words: "What you put your trust in makes all the difference in whether you roll with the punches or buckle under the pressure."

Gretchen knew that she had been placing her trust in the wrong things. Bowing her head, she spent the next few moments asking God to walk with her through the long, painful months of recovery. Immediately, she felt His loving presence fill the room.

Are you placing your trust in the right things or the wrong things?

---

**FAITH IS TRUST THAT'S BEEN PUT TO THE TEST.**

---

*My soul is downcast within me;*
*therefore I will remember you.*

**PSALM 42:6**

---

*"With the loving mercy of our God, a*
*new day from heaven will dawn upon*
*us. It will shine on those who live in*
*darkness, in the shadow of death. It*
*will guide us into the path of peace."*

**LUKE 1:78-79 NCV**

---

*When you go through deep waters*
*and great trouble, I will be with you.*
*When you go through rivers of*
*difficulty, you will not drown! When you*
*walk through the fire of oppression,*
*you will not be burned up—the flames*
*will not consume you.*

**ISAIAH 43:2 TLB**

# FOREVER BLESSED

Depression had been part of Dorothy's life as far back as she could remember. Even when nothing was really wrong, she still felt as if something just wasn't right. For several years she'd been on antidepressants and had spent time with a therapist. There had even been times when she had taken a leave of absence from her teaching career.

After a period of time, Dorothy's fellow teachers noticed that she seemed to have a newfound joy, even on days when the classroom seemed like a war zone. When they asked what had made the change in her life, Dorothy couldn't help but talk about her "blessings" book.

"Every morning I spend some time reading the Psalms," Dorothy explained. "I can relate to all those emotional ups and downs. Then, I write down in my journal everything I'm thankful for. If it's a tough morning, I go back through the pages and read what God has done for me in the past. That always brings to mind something new I need to say 'thank You' for. Those few moments with God give me the courage to face the day with a positive outlook."

Consider starting a "blessings" book of your own.

COUNTING YOUR BLESSINGS DIVIDES YOUR SORROW.

*The Lord looks down and sees all mankind.*

**PSALM 33:13**

---

*"Yes, be bold and strong! Banish fear and doubt! For remember, the Lord your God is with you wherever you go."*

**JOSHUA 1:9 TLB**

---

*God did not give us a spirit that makes us afraid but a spirit of power and love and self-control.*

**2 TIMOTHY 1:7 NCV**

# LOST IN THE CROWD

Going back to school had never been part of Rhonda's grand scheme for life, but there she was. After her husband left her. she felt lost. "His" plans had always been "their" plans. Now, she had to make plans of her own. But the classrooms in college didn't feel as friendly as they did in high school. She not only felt alone, she felt almost invisible.

But she knew she wasn't. She knew God was by her side. She pictured Him walking beside her into class or sitting in the car with her as she drove to campus. The more she shared her heart with Him, the nearer she felt His presence.

Taking it one day at a time, Rhonda found herself making friends, and soon she was fully enjoying her new educational challenge. Glimpses of God in her quiet time with Him each morning gave her the courage she needed to pursue a teaching career.

Is there an unexpected challenge in your life? Reach out to God—He's always there for you.

COURAGE IS THE POWER TO LET GO OF THE FAMILIAR.

*On my bed I remember you; I think of you through the watches of the night.*

**PSALM 63:6**

---

*It is in vain that you rise up early and go late to rest, eating the bread of anxious toil; for he gives to his beloved sleep.*

**PSALM 127:2 RSV**

---

*I go to bed and sleep in peace, because, Lord, only you keep me safe.*

**PSALM 4:8 NCV**

# NIGHT WATCH

*D*eeper and deeper budget cuts within my school system. Some of my coworkers have already lost their positions and student/teacher ratios continue to increase. More layoffs, they'd said. What if they let me go? How are we going to pay off this house? We can barely afford it. Every night was the same. Greg tossed and turned until the early hours of the morning, then woke up exhausted the next day.

Finally a friend suggested that Greg pray whenever he couldn't sleep. "If you fall asleep, God won't be offended, and if you stay awake, at least you're talking to Someone who can actually help you," Steve suggested.

So Greg took his advice. Once he got into the habit of nightly conversations with his Creator, he began looking forward to bedtime. Most nights, he fell asleep after a few words of thanks. But when sleep still eluded him, Greg found comfort in knowing he wasn't alone. Those few moments with God made all the difference, and each day he rejoiced because he still had a job at the school.

Do you spend your nights tossing and turning? Give God your troubles, and get some sleep!

> GIVE YOUR TROUBLES TO GOD; HE WILL BE UP
> ALL NIGHT ANYWAY.

*Whatever you do, do it all for the glory of God.*

**1 CORINTHIANS 10:31**

---

*God is not unfair. He will not forget how hard you have worked for Him and how you have shown your love to Him by caring for other Christians, as you still do.*

**HEBREWS 6:10 NLT**

---

*Whatever your hand finds to do, do it with your might.*

**ECCLESIASTES 9:10 NKJV**

# JUST A DISHWASHER

"Thanks a lot." Though he was smiling, the sarcasm dripped off Jerry's lips nearly as heavily as the soapy water dripped off his apron. Three racks of dirty dishes now blocked his exit from the kitchen. This isn't the life I dreamed of, he thought. *As a teacher I wanted to make a difference in students' lives.*

Jerry has been forced to take a second job during the summer to make ends meet. A baking pan slipped into the sink, splashing hot, sudsy water onto his apron. He could feel it soaking through his clothes, but he kept on working. He scrubbed until the pots and pans were cleaner than they'd ever been.

"Jerry," the kitchen manager said, "I just wanted to tell you how much I appreciate your attitude. You don't complain, you do good work . . . and you make my day better. Thanks."

Jerry paused for a moment and smiled. *With God's help, dishwashers can make a difference too*, he thought.

Are you doing your best, right where you are?

---

**EVERY CALLING IS GREAT WHEN GREATLY PURSUED.**

---

*You have made known to me the path of life; you will fill me with joy in your presence, with eternal pleasures at your right hand.*

**PSALM 16:11**

---

*I will instruct you and teach you in the way you should go; I will guide you with My eye.*

**PSALM 32:8 NKJV**

---

*The purpose in a man's mind is like deep water, but a man of will draw it out.*

**PROVERBS 20:5 RSV**

# WALKING A NEW ROAD

A mid the party horns, music, and laughter, Donna looked back over the past twenty years of teaching. Though her coworkers insisted on telling and retelling the story of her first day at Elton High—and what became known as "The Last Teacher Standing"—Donna's recollection landed on the day before she started her job.

It was a Sunday, and Donna was sitting where she always sat on Sunday mornings—on a cold, hard pew in church. But this Sunday was different. For the first time in her young life, she really "got it." She understood this "God thing" as she'd referred to it so many times before. And what a change it had made! It was a beginning and a direction she never would have anticipated.

As she blew out the candles on the layers of the book-shaped cake, Helen silently thanked God that she'd seen the signpost reading, "This way."

God wants to be involved in the everyday moments of your life. Will you let Him?

---

FAITH WEARS EVERYDAY CLOTHES AND PROVES HERSELF IN LIFE'S ORDINARY SITUATIONS.

*"In the image of God has God made man."*

**GENESIS 9:6**

---

*Jacob said, "No, I pray you, if I have found favor in your sight, then accept my present from my hand; for truly to see your face is like seeing the face of God, with such favor have you received me."*

**GENESIS 33:10 RSV**

---

*But as it is written: "Eye has not seen, nor ear heard, Nor have entered into the heart of man The things which God has prepared for those who love Him." But God has revealed them to us through His Spirit. For the Spirit searches all things, yes, the deep things of God.*

**1 CORINTHIANS 2:9-10 NKJV**

# GLIMPSES OF AN INVISIBLE GOD

"Spending time with God isn't as easy as it sounds," Tyler, one of Sarah's fifth-grade students at Brighton Bible School, told her. "It's hard to carry on a conversation with Someone you can't see."

"But you can see Him," Sarah replied, "if you are looking through the eyes of faith. We can catch glimpses of God every day as we look around us at the things He has created. Most clearly, we can see Him as we look at each other, for we alone of all His creation have been made in His own image. Of course God is perfect." she continued, "and human beings clearly aren't. But at least we know that He created us to be very much like himself. In that way, we can see Him with our hearts."

"Thanks, Ms. Green," Tyler said. "I think I just saw a glimpse of God in you!"

Look around. You're bound to see God's image in those around you.

MAN IS HEAVEN'S MASTERPIECE.

*I will sing to the Lord, for he has been good to me.*

**PSALM 13:6**

---

*Whatever you do or say, let it be as a representative of the Lord Jesus, and come with him into the presence of God the Father to give him your thanks.*

**COLOSSIANS 3:17 TLB**

---

*Yes, they shall sing of the ways of the Lord, for great is the glory of the Lord.*

**PSALM 138:5 NKJV**

# TRAFFIC JAM

Rush hour traffic only added to Helen's frustration. By the time she arrived in the school parking lot, she had to bite her lip to control the angry words on her mind. By lunchtime, she'd relaxed a bit, but all too soon it was time to drive home. Dinner hour with her family was usually far from pleasant, and Helen knew something had to change. So she started with the dial on her radio.

She had always felt worship songs should be reserved for church. But when a new Christian radio station started up, promising music with a "positive" message, she decided to try it out for a few days. By the end of the week, her absent-minded humming had turned into full-blown singing. And she sensed God listening in. Occasionally, drivers stuck in traffic next to her did a double-take. But usually, they just smiled. And Helen found herself smiling back.

Do you need an attitude change at work, at home, on the highway? Maybe you should discover the daily benefits of worship.

---

**WORSHIP RENEWS THE SPIRIT AS SLEEP RENEWS THE BODY.**

*Whatever you do, work at it with all your heart, as working for the Lord, not for men.*

## COLOSSIANS 3:23

---

*For I know the plans I have for you, says the Lord. They are plans for good and not for evil, to give you a future and a hope.*

## JEREMIAH 29:11

---

*"Do not labor for food which perishes, but for the food which endures to everlasting life, which the Son of Man will give you, because God the Father has set His seal on Him."*

## JOHN 6:27 NKJV

# NO LABOR LOST

Shannon walked to the back entrance of the library. *Even if I walked through the front door, people wouldn't really see me*, she thought. After all, she was just a student-teacher. The work was hard, and there was no pay, but it was required to fulfill her graduation requirements to become a certified teacher.

Each day, Donna's work began before she opened the door to the library. As she walked through the parking lot each morning, she put her day into God's hands. She prayed for His strength, joy, and perspective. As she worked, she pretended she was teaching God's students. At quitting time, Donna was always proud of what she'd accomplished. And she felt sure her Heavenly Father was too.

Have you placed your day in God's hands?

> A TASK WITHOUT A VISION IS DRUDGERY; A VISION WITHOUT A TASK IS A DREAM; A TASK WITH A VISION IS VICTORY.

*All who humble themselves before the Lord shall be given every blessing, and shall have wonderful peace.*

**PSALM 37:11 TLB**

---

*The humble He guides injustice, and the humble He teaches His way.*

**PSALM 25:9 NKJV**

---

*"Therefore, anyone who becomes as humble as this little child is the greatest in the Kingdom of Heaven."*

**MATTHEW 18:4 NLT**

# CURTAIN CALL

**W**ithout a word, Lorna turned and headed back to the dressing room. She'd seen the cast list for the drama department's latest production. Another show put together without her input. The head of the department never allowed her to help in decision-making, although the lead players were her own students.

Bitter tears coursed down, her cheeks. She'd worked hard with these students to bring them to a higher level. She'd been successful. That was obvious in the department head's decision to put her team on top.

Lorna angrily told God how unfair her current situation was, how her talent was being wasted, and how she deserved more. But as God's peace came over her, she also glimpsed His perspective—how any talent she had was a gift from Him and how her hurt stemmed from pride, not injustice. In a few God moments, Lorna found herself in need of forgiveness—as well as strength and inspiration to continue to give her best to her students.

Ground is *never* lost when you commit yourself to God.

---

TALENT IS GOD-GIVEN; BE THANKFUL.
CONCEIT IS SELF-GIVEN; BE CAREFUL.

---

*God has been gracious to me and I have all I need.*

**GENESIS 33:11**

---

*It is he who will supply all your needs from his riches in glory, because of what Christ Jesus has done for us.*

**PHILIPPIANS 4:19 TLB**

---

*The blessing of the Lord makes one rich, and He adds no sorrow with it.*

**PROVERBS 10:22 NKJV**

# ENOUGH STUFF

The junk drawer was stuck again. "You're right, Helen. We *do* need new kitchen cabinets, " Jim called out. He silently added "remodel kitchen" to the growing list of things they couldn't afford on his teaching salary. Then he began pushing and pulling the drawer, which eventually gave way. Paper clips, old candies, pins, movie stubs, broken pencils, nonworking pens, and many other unidentifiable objects spilled onto the linoleum.

Jim scanned the debris field, looking for anything of value. He found nothing. He looked around the kitchen — at the stove with two working burners, the refrigerator half-filled with food. Then he looked into the family room at another debris field — this one caused by a now-napping two-year-old tornado. He heard Helen moving about in the other room. And he smiled.

Jim stopped worrying about what they couldn't afford. He had all he desired — and more. Bowing his head, he took a moment to thank God for his many blessings.

Have you thanked God for your blessings today?

IT'S POSSIBLE TO BECOME SO BUSY ADDING UP YOUR TROUBLES THAT YOU FORGET TO COUNT YOUR BLESSINGS.

*We fix our eyes not on what is seen, but on what is unseen. For what is seen is temporary, but what is unseen in eternal.*

## 2 CORINTHIANS 4:18

---

*Just as you trusted Christ to save you, trust him, too, for each day's problems; live in vital union with him.*

## COLOSSIANS 2:6 TLB

---

*Whatever is born of God overcomes the world; and this is the victory that overcomes the world, our faith.*

## 1 JOHN 5:4 RSV

# THE REST OF THE STORY

She saw the other children stare when Sammy climbed onto the slide. She'd heard it all before: the whispers and, occasionally, the taunts—from children as well as adults. Beth knew what they saw: an awkward kid with Down's syndrome. But she saw a fun-loving, tenderhearted twelve-year-old student. She saw the face of a special education student she dearly loved.

"What we see with our eyes, whether it's a person or a circumstance," Beth told a friend, "doesn't tell the whole story. Only God knows what's going on behind the scenes. And often, that's the most important part."

Each time Beth looked at her special student, she understood that God had taken a child whom others viewed as a tragedy and made him a source of daily victories. Beth prayed daily for Sammy, and she knew as long as she kept her eyes fixed on God, He would help her to teach Sammy everything he needed to learn from her this school year.

Whatever your circumstances, trust them to God. Soon you will be seeing what others do not—the rest of the story from God's perspective.

> GOD REVEALS TO THE HEART WHAT CAN'T BE SEEN WITH THE EYES.

*They waited for me as for showers and drank in my words as the spring rain.*

**JOB 29:23**

---

*If you want to know what God wants you to do, ask him, and he will gladly tell you, for he is always ready to give a bountiful supply of wisdom to all who ask him; he will not resent it.*

**JAMES 1:5 TLB**

---

*The Lord grants wisdom! From His mouth come knowledge and understanding.*

**PROVERBS 2:6 NLT**

# SHARED WISDOM

The diverse group of teenagers sat in rapt attention while Jason spoke. He'd often felt successful in leading his class discussions, but he also knew even the best teachers couldn't expect to "connect" with each student every day.

His students asked lots of questions: things that made Jason smile . . . and things that made his heart heavy. But they continued to ask, and he continued to trust God for the answers that the textbooks couldn't provide.

As he drove home from school that afternoon, he felt a sense of awe as he reflected on God's faithfulness. He knew that unless God empowered his words, they would simply be just that—words, unable to impact the life of even one young person. In that moment, he acknowledged his utter dependence on God and thanked Him for allowing him to be part of his students' lives and God's wonderful plan.

God wants to empower your words as you teach students. Will you let Him?

> TO HAVE FAITH IS TO BELIEVE THE TASK AHEAD OF US IS NEVER AS GREAT AS HE POWER BEHIND US.

*"Before they call I will answer; while they are still speaking I will hear."*

**ISAIAH 65:24**

---

*Therefore I say to you, do not worry about your life. . . . "Look at the birds of the air, for they neither sow nor reap nor gather into barns; yet your heavenly Father feeds them. Are you not of more value than they?"*

**MATTHEW 6:25-26 NKJV**

---

*'You shall not go out in haste, and you shall not go in flight, for the LORD will go before you, and the God of Israel will be your rear guard."*

**ISAIAH 52:12 RSV**

# GIFTS OF LOVE

Chris set the mail on the table, unopened. What was the point? It was just more bills. The occasional advertisement only reminded him of what he and his family couldn't afford. Budget cuts to an already small teaching salary had set him back financially.

As he turned to leave the kitchen, a hand-addressed envelope caught his eye. He tore it open, and a folded sheet of paper fell onto the table. It read simply, "God brought you to mind today." Tucked inside was a money order, enough to pay for rent and then some. Stunned, Chris remembered his disheartened prayer of just an hour before, asking God for help. He now realized that God's answer to his prayer was in the works even before the words crossed his lips.

It wasn't something he did very often. But words of thanks and praise instantly overflowed from his grateful heart.

Remember, it takes only a glimpse of an invisible God to change everything.

---

**NEVER BE AFRAID TO TRUST AN UNKNOWN FUTURE TO A KNOWN GOD.**

*Invigorate my soul so I can praise you well, use your decrees to put iron in my soul.*

**PSALM 119:175 MSG**

---

*He gives power to the faint, and to him who has no might he increases strength.*

**ISAIAH 40:29 RSV**

---

*He restores my soul.*

**PSALM 23:3 NKJV**

# IGNITED HEART

D on was exhausted. Time on the road with the drivers' education students had taken its toll. He was supposed to go to a Wednesday night church service, but what he really wanted was to turn on the TV, surf, and fall asleep. Then the phone rang. It was Eric, wanting a ride to church. Reluctantly, he agreed.

As Don drove to Eric's apartment, he began to regret his decision. "I'm beat. Don't think I'll be staying," he said to him. "You'll need to find a different ride home." But as they pulled up to the church, Don decided he'd step in for a minute.

Two hours later, he sought out Eric who, perplexed, said, "Thought you were going home."

Don replied, "I was wrong. I think I was more empty than tired—and setting aside a little time to spend with my Maker was the perfect filling station."

God wants to fill you to overflowing. Will you let Him?

OUR WEAKNESS MAKES US APPRECIATE GOD'S STRENGTH.

*There is a way that seems right to a man, But its end is the way of death.*

**PROVERBS 14:12 NKJV**

---

*"Then I will lead the blind along a way they never knew; I will guide them along paths they have not known. I will make the darkness become light for them, and the rough ground smooth. These are the things I will do; I will not leave my people."*

**ISAIAH 42:16 NCV**

---

*Yea, thou art my rock and my fortress; for thy name's sake lead me and guide me.*

**PSALM 31:3 RSV**

# WRONG TURN

In a split second Hank realized there was not a thing he could do. His truck was going to slide right through the stop sign in front of the high school. He turned the steering wheel hard to the right, praying his tires would find something other than solid ice beneath them. The truck hit a patch of blacktop and careened into the curb nearly hitting a school bus. *They should have cancelled school today*, the music teacher thought.

After a few false starts, Hank finally pulled into his favorite spot next to the gym. When he applied the brakes, his truck pulled hard to the right. *So much for putting off that realignment*, he thought.

Like Hank's truck, when we are inattentive to our spiritual lives, we screech and bump along the road of life (if we're on the right road at all). The great thing is, spiritual realignment requires no money. It's the result of an open Bible and open communication with God. What about you? Do you need a realignment? It's free.

IT IS RIGHT THAT YOU SHOULD BEGIN AGAIN EVERY DAY. THERE IS NO BETTER WAY TO FINISH THE SPIRITUAL THAN TO BE EVER BEGINNING.

*Whoever would draw near to God must believe that he exists and that he rewards those who seek him.*

**HEBREWS 11:6 RSV**

---

*Create in me a clean heart, O God; and renew a right spirit within me.*

**PSALM 51:10 KJV**

---

*I call to the Lord, who is worthy of praise, and I am saved from my enemies.*

**PSALM 18:3 NIV**

# NEXT TO NOTHING

How do you find a path to God when you live on a self-made "island"? Paula began to retrace her steps of faith. "There is no God. I am certain of it," she used to say. Friends gradually dwindled because of her arrogance. When she had ostracized the most patient of her friends, Hannah, a kindergarten teacher across the hall, her retreat to the "island" was complete.

"No one can bother me now. No one can tell me lies about God anymore," she said. Yet time began to eat away at Paula. She was safe from "harm," but she was lonely. The first sighting of a "ship in the distance" resembled Hannah. She'd come back to offer a renewal of friendship. Then others came with open arms. Perhaps they'd never left.

In a moment she could only construe as a "miracle," Paula finally understood. Was it something Hannah had said or something she had learned as a child? She was never quite sure what brought her down this path—but she did know one thing. *There is a God. I am certain of it . . . because I have met Him.*

HE WHO CREATED US WITHOUT OUR HELP WILL NOT SAVE US WITHOUT OUR CONSENT.

*The memory of the righteous will be a blessing.*

**PROVERBS 10:7**

---

*When pride comes, then comes shame; but with the lowly is wisdom.*

**PROVERBS 11:2 KJV**

---

*God can use sorrow in our lives to help us turn away from sin and seek salvation. We will never regret that kind of sorrow. But sorrow without repentance is the kind that results in death.*

**2 CORINTHIANS 7:10 NLT**

# ERASING REGRET

"Looking out for number one" was Phil's motto. It had worked well in securing him a coaching position in a big 6A school, a house in a very respectable neighborhood, as well as an enviable spot at most sports events in town. But it couldn't secure him peace of mind. His "it's all about me" lifestyle left him with few friends, alimony payments, and regrets.

Of course, he'd never say that to anyone at school. But lately, Phil found himself saying it aloud in the empty hallways of his home. The surprising thing was that he felt as though Someone was actually listening. Could that Someone be God? he wondered one day. And deep inside, that same day, Someone whispered, "Yes." And everything changed.

Doing the right thing today comes with a lifetime bonus-blessing in place of regret. That's because today's decisions are tomorrow's memories. And not all memories are worth cherishing. God's forgiveness can help erase regret. But why not stop it before it starts?

THE MAN WHO HAS UNDERSTANDING HAS EVERYTHING.

*This god is our God for ever and ever;*
*he will be our guide even to the end.*

**PSALM 48:14**

---

*Plans fail without good advice, but they*
*succeed with the advice of many others.*

**PROVERBS 15:22 NCV**

---

*"I will always show you where to go.*
*I'll give you a full life in the emptiest*
*of places—firm muscles, strong bones.*
*You'll be like a well-watered garden,*
*a gurgling spring that never runs dry."*

**ISAIAH 58:11 MSG**

# WHAT SHOULD I DO?

The land of opportunity was filled with question marks. *What should I do? Where should I go?* Kim wondered. While teaching Chinese at a big city college, he often stared at the globe. He'd trace with a finger the path he'd taken to the United States. "It is a great land . . . but there are many land mines," his mother had warned him.

The college dean, Jack, and his wife, Kate, had been terrific hosts. They looked after Kim as if he were their own son. But whenever he asked for direction, they responded with the question: "What do you think is right?" Kim didn't know the answer. He felt he couldn't trust his own mind because it seemed to change with the direction of the wind.

Then his friend Linda told him about the Bible. "Take a look," she'd said. "It is a book of great wisdom." He buried himself in its pages and became saturated in its wisdom. Then one day he asked Linda how to meet the Author of this wisdom. Kim doesn't fear questions anymore—they always lead him back to God.

What about you? Let your questions lead you to the One with the answers.

GOD REVEALS HIMSELF UNFAILINGLY TO THE
THOUGHTFUL SEEKER.

*Without having seen him you love him; though you do not now see him you believe in him and rejoice with unutterable and exalted joy.*

**1 PETER 1:8 RSV**

---

*What is faith? It is the confident assurance that something we want is going to happen. It is the certainty that what we hope for is waiting for us, even though we cannot see it up ahead.*

**HEBREWS 11:1 TLB**

---

*We walk by faith, not by sight.*

**2 CORINTHIANS 5:7 NKJV**

# YOU'VE GOT MAIL

In many ways, Ben's romance with Wendy mirrored his relationship with God. When he first met her, he was at his computer desk typing away in a chat room about the merits of his favorite modern jazz artists. The most articulate comments came from a newcomer to the room who went by PANFRIEND.

It wasn't until a few weeks later that Ben discovered PANFRIEND wasn't a comment on Wendy's interest in cooking, but rather a reference to James Barrie's famous novel. She was a teacher who loved children and children's books. As in his relationship with God, Ben couldn't see the person on the other side of the modem. But he got to know her and, in time, learned to trust her.

The day they met in person—at an amusement park in California—was magical. As they rode the roller coaster, they somehow knew their life together would have its sharp turns and surprises but that they'd do all right in the end.

> THE SECRET OF POWER IN OUR LIVES IS TO KNOW GOD AND EXPECT GREAT THINGS FROM HIM.

*"Blessed are those who have not seen and yet have believed."*

**JOHN 20:29 RSV**

*We were saved in this hope, but hope that is seen is not hope; for why does one still hope for what he sees? But if we hope for what we do not see, we eagerly wait for it with perseverance.*

**ROMANS 8:24-25 NKJV**

*If you go the wrong way—to the right or to the left—you will hear a voice behind you saying, "This is the right way. You should go this way."*

**ISAIAH 30:21 NCV**

# OUT OF THE DARK

Walking to class with Erica was a learning experience for Jane. Erica followed the sidewalk and knew exactly when to cross. Then when they got to Erica's classroom, Erica knew where to find her desk and teaching tools.

Twice a week Erica taught a night class. Not that it was much different from the day for her because she was blind. One such late evening, Erica and Jane paused to go their separate ways down the hall. Suddenly the lights went out. Jane froze, but Erica kept moving. "I know where the doorways are," she'd said, tugging on Jane's sleeve.

A few nights later, Jane sat in her living room, plaintively asking the same question she asked every night since Erica had told her about God. "How can I believe a God I can't see?" Then, while glancing at her TV dinner, she understood! She remembered Erica's words: "I know where the nothing else, doorways are."

Instinctively, lane knew where God was too.

---

AS HE THAT FEARS GOD FEARS NOTHING ELSE, SO HE THAT SEES GOD SEES EVERYTHING ELSE.

*Search me, O God, and know my heart; test me and know my anxious thoughts.*

**PSALM 139:23**

---

*Then you called out to God in your desperate condition; he got you out in the nick of time. He quieted the wind down to a whisper, put a muzzle on all the big waves. And you were so glad when the storm died down, and he led you safely back to harbor.*

**PSALM 107:20-30 MSG**

---

*Those who trust in the Lord are like Mount Zion, which cannot be moved, but abides forever.*

**PSALM 125:1 NKJV**

# RUNNING ON EMPTY

Tara was late — again. She ran out the front door, clumsily pulling on her coat while clenching a hurriedly buttered bagel between her teeth. As her car screeched out of the driveway, Tara began rehearsing her apology and her excuses. How could she convince her students they needed to arrive on time if the teacher was always late?

Tara reached for her tape of tropical rain forest sounds to help calm her jagged nerves. She turned the screeching monkeys and cascading waterfall up loud enough to drown out the car's racing engine. Suddenly, WHAM! Everything in the car, including Tara, jolted with a sudden impact.

That stupid speed bump, she thought. Why do I always forget it's there when I'm in a hurry? She slowed down and saw a cat saunter across the drive. I could have hit him, she realized, suddenly glad for the bump.

Not every inconvenience is a random annoyance. Sometimes, God throws a speed bump into your life to get your attention or slow you down.

> BEWARE OF THE BARRENNESS OF A BUSY LIFE.

*"Why do you look at the speck of sawdust in your brother's eye and pay no attention to the plank in your own eye?"*

**MATTHEW 7:3**

---

*In the mouth of the foolish is a rod of pride: but the lips of the wise shall preserve them.*

**PROVERBS 14:3 KJV**

---

*Pride leads to arguments; those who take advice are wise.*

**PROVERBS 13:10 NLT**

# TUNNEL VISION

Joe's Bible was tucked in a drawer in his desk, ready to be pulled out if a student needed help. His prayer journal was hardbound and he entered his prayers and also wrote probing questions to search his heart and make sure he was not allowing secret sin to taint his life or his interactions with students. He wasn't an eloquent prayer, but he presented his requests in simple language and told God honestly what was on his mind.

Joe didn't comment on others' weaknesses, but if they asked his advice he had a Bible verse that often gave them hope and lit their way out of difficulty. And he was quick to take advice. His own prayer book was a record of his own struggles, so he never jumped on anyone for theirs, even if they were irritating to him. Joe struggled to grow in Jesus' love, and he was finding that the time he spent with God was changing him somehow. He felt the pride of his youth melting away and something—was it humility?—taking its place.

Do you struggle with pride and a critical spirit? Let God melt that away for you and replace it with a loving, humble heart.

PRIDE IS SPIRITUAL CANCER; IT EATS THE VERY POSSIBILITY OF LOVE OR CONTENTMENT, OR EVEN COMMON SENSE.

*The smallness you feel comes from within you. Your lives aren't small, but you're living them in a small way.*

**2 CORINTHIANS 6:12 MSG**

*Two are better than one; because they have a good reward for their labour. For if they fall, the one will lift up his fellow: but woe to him that is alone when he falleth; for he hath not another to help him up. Again, if two lie together, then they have heat: but how can one be warm alone? And if one prevail against him, two shall withstand him; and a threefold cord is not quickly broken.*

**ECCLESIASTES 4:9-12 KJV**

*God sets the lonely in families, he leads forth the prisoners with singing.*

**PSALM 68:6**

# SMALL WORLD?

Byron rarely ventured outside of his house. After a hard day of teaching history at the high school, he would retire to the easy chair in front of the TV. He didn't dislike his neighbors; he simply hadn't ever met them.

Byron enjoyed his world. It was familiar and relatively risk-free. He knew just what to expect every day. Then something happened that allowed him to meet all his neighbors—nearly all at once—in a way he could have never imagined. Byron lost his house to a fire. As a result, he met the Johnson family, who had just lost a son to cancer; the Kyles, whose family was torn apart by divorce; Mabel Thornberry, who had just retired after thirty-seven years of teaching; and the Lamonts—his next-door neighbors with whom he had never had even one real conversation.

When the fire occurred and all was lost, Bryon thought his life would disappear too. Instead, it just got bigger—much, much bigger.

YOUR NEIGHBOR IS THE MAN WHO NEEDS YOU.

*Long before he laid down earth's foundations, he had us in mind, had settled on us as the focus of his love.*

**EPHESIANS 1:4-MSG**

---

*"You did not choose me, but I chose you and appointed you that you should go and bear fruit and that your fruit should abide; so that whatever you ask the Father in my name, he may give it to you."*

**JOHN 15:16 RSV**

---

*We have the mind of Christ.*

**1 CORINTHIANS 2:16 RSV**

# WHO AM I?

Cyril's goal was to search as far back in history as existing records would take him and map out his family tree. After years of research, he traced his family back to the seventeenth century. Proud of his work, he presented his findings to a local museum. Though initially impressed, the museum's curator, an expert in genealogy, eventually discovered an error in Cyril's work around the turn of the twentieth century.

Cyril was crushed. Overreacting to this discovery, he became sullen and depressed. Although the librarian at a large high school and a well-respected instructor at the college in research development, he cried, "Once again, I don't know who I am."

Discovering your genealogy can be interesting and challenging—but it doesn't shape your identity. You are a unique creation of God. You can honor His creativity by becoming wholly aware of and content with the person He has made you to be.

TO KNOW MAN WE MUST BEGIN WITH GOD.

*Speak to one another with psalms, hymns and spiritual songs. Sing and make music in your heart to the Lord.*

**EPHESIANS 5:19**

---

*A servant of the Lord must not quarrel but be gentle to all.*

**2 TIMOTHY 2:24 NKJV**

---

*May the God of steadfastness and encouragement grant you to live in such harmony with one another, in accord with Christ Jesus, that together you may with one voice glorify the God and Father of our Lord Jesus Christ.*

**ROMANS 15:5-6 RSV**

# ONE LITTLE VOICE

Sometimes they called the yelling "disagreements." Sometimes they called it "differing opinions." But rarely did they call it what it was: screaming. Nancy and Frank, both educators at a private institution, loved their family. They simply disagreed — loudly — on how to deal with their teenager Ray. 'He needs a stricter set of rules!" yelled Frank.

"What he needs is to be allowed to fail!" yelled Nancy.

Ray's younger brother, Kyle, didn't like the yelling. He knew his parents loved each other — they said so often — but he wanted them to stop fighting. One day, during a shouting match, Kyle quietly opened his bedroom door and sang a song his parents had taught him: "Keep on the sunny side, always on the sunny side." The yelling stopped.

By the time Frank and Nancy walked into his room, Kyle was singing low in his sweet five-year-old voice, but the message still rang loud and clear. "I think God is trying to tell us something," said Frank.

Nancy smiled, tears in her eyes, "Yes, out of the mouth of a babe."

Keep your ears open. God may speak to you through your children or students.

---

DO WE STOP AND THINK BEFORE WE SPEAK, CONSIDERING THE POTENCY OF THE PHRASES WE UTTER?

*Pray every way you know how, for everyone you know.*

**1 TIMOTHY 2:1 MSG**

---

*The Lord sees the good people and listens to their prayers.*

**1 PETER 3:12 NCV**

---

*The Spirit helps us in our weakness; for we do not know how to pray as we ought, but the Spirit himself intercedes for us with sighs too deep for words. And he who searches the hearts of men knows what is the mind of the Spirit, because the Spirit intercedes for the saints according to the will of God.*

**ROMANS 8:26-27 RSV**

# FROM THE HEART

"How, uh ,. . . how do you pray?" John asked his friend Tim sheepishly. "The only prayer I know is the 'Our Father,' but I don't always feel like I'm really talking to God." When John had first met his new colleague and team-teaching partner, Tim, he thought he was strange. Tim talked about God, and talked to God, as if He were a member of his family. To John, God was a distant figure whose attention you could rarely get.

"Well, John, some people say specific prayers, like the 'Our Father,' which Jesus gave to His disciples as a model of prayer. And it's good to pray using that model, but God is a Heavenly Father who wants to hear from His children—the same way you like to hear from each of your own children. You'd want to know if your son had a bad day or if something good happened. And you also probably wouldn't mind hearing him tell you that he loves you."

That day, John, a devoted dad, began to understand how to relate to his devoted Father in Heaven. After that, God began to seem very personal and close to him.

PRAYER IS SIMPLE, AS SIMPLE AS A CHILD MAKING KNOWN ITS WANTS TO ITS PARENTS.

*The day for building your walls will come, the day for extending your boundaries.*

**MICAH 7:11**

---

*Overwhelming victory is ours through Christ who loved us enough to die for us.*

**ROMANS 8:37 TLB**

---

*With the LORD on my side I do not fear. What can man do to me?*

**PSALM 118:6 RSV**

# SPHERE

For seven years Michelle took care of her two small children at home. Her sphere of influence included only seven-year-old Mandy and four-year-old Isaac. She could quote from just about any children's television program and knew each storybook character on a first-name basis.

When it came to conversing with adults, however, she was a little out of practice. She'd chat with a neighbor once in a while. Mostly, though, she talked with little people who had sticky' fingers and milk mustaches. So when she decided to return to the classroom to instruct college freshmen, she knew it would be a challenge she couldn't meet without help. So she prayed.

It was a challenge—for the first few days, anyway. She quickly learned to avoid the habit of adding "y" to the end of words as in, "My computer 'mousey' doesn't seem to work." Within a couple weeks, she was doing just fine. And even better, she was making a difference in the lives of people over four feet tall. But best of all was the way she saw God smoothing all kinds of circumstances for her in order to make it possible for her to succeed—and to succeed with ease.

Is God asking you to step out of your comfort zone? Trust Him to smooth the way.

---

COURAGE IS THE STRENGTH OR CHOICE TO BEGIN A CHANGE. DETERMINATION IS THE PERSISTENCE TO CONTINUE IN THAT CHANGE.

---

*Is anyone thirsty? Come! All who will, come and drink, drink freely of the Water of Life!*

**REVELATION 22:17 MSG**

---

*Dear brothers, is your life full of difficulties and temptations? Then be happy, for when the way is rough, your patience has a chance to grow. So let it grow, and don't try to squirm out of your problems. For when your patience is finally in full bloom, then you will be ready for anything, strong in character, full and complete.*

**JAMES 1:2-4 TLB**

---

*You have need of endurance, so that you may do the will of God and receive what is promised.*

**HEBREWS 10:36 RSV**

# FILL 'ER UP!

"**I**'m thirsty!" Suddenly, Alec's statement had morphed into a command. "I want a drink right now!"

Amy glanced in the rearview mirror and said, "Alec, I told you that you're going to have to wait a little while longer. We're almost home." Her three-year-old said nothing . . . for about thirty seconds. Then the "I'm thirsty" tirade began again.

When they got home from Amy's back-to-school night, memories of new parents, her neatly decorated classrooms, and fifteen little hugs and a firm handshake faded as Amy raced to the kitchen and filled a cup with water for him. Two small sips later, he set the cup on the counter. "Thanks, Mom." Two sips? That was it? she thought. All that complaining, and he took just two sips?

"Don't you want any more?" she asked.

"Nope."

Amy couldn't relate to "two sips" of anything — particularly when it came to God's "well." Daily, she would go and ask God for a bucketful of patience; He certainly never had to ask, "Don't you want any more?"

Just then, Alec called, "I want juice!" They were out of juice. But Amy was glad that God's well never ran dry.

> BE PATIENT WITH EVERYONE, BUT ABOVE ALL WITH YOURSELF.

*Thou wilt keep him in perfect peace, whose mind is stayed on thee: because he trusteth in thee.*

**ISAIAH 26:3 KJV**

---

*You give peace of mind to all who love Your law. Nothing can make them fall.*

**PSALM 119:165 CEV**

---

*"Then words of praise will be on their lips. May they have peace, both near and far, for I will heal them all," says the Lord.*

**ISAIAH 57:19 NLT**

# SEEKING PEACE

ngela had a tumultuous childhood. She never knew her father; and her mother led a nomadic life, moving from job to job, town to town, and man to man. As an adult, Angela faced great insecurities and self-doubt as she struggled to face her first-grade class and the many moods of their parents.

One day, the principal's secretary, Dana, asked her to take a walk with her during their lunch hour. "Only God can give you peace," Dana said. "He is what you have been searching for."

Angela gave her life and her past to God that day, and for the first time she experienced a deep and lasting peace. When the old insecurities and self-doubt try to sneak back in during her prep time, she closes her eyes and waits quietly in God's presence until she feels settled and calm once more.

If you need peace today, open your heart. It will take only a few moments with God to establish peace in your life.

BEING AT PEACE WITH YOURSELF IS A DIRECT
RESULT OF FINDING PEACE WITH GOD.

*Now we ask you, brothers, to respect those who work hard among you, who are over you in the Lord and who admonish you.*

**1 THESSALONIANS 5:12**

---

*People who despise advice will find themselves in trouble; those who respect it will succeed.*

**PROVERBS 13:13 NLT**

---

*Out of respect for Christ, be courteously reverent to one another.*

**EPHESIANS 5:21 MSG**

# WHO'S THE BOSS?

Principal Thomas was a commanding presence, not because of his impressive height, but because of his focused vision. He was admired for his passion—but that passion often carried on and on in meetings, causing the faculty and staff to be late to class or late for after-school appointments and family time. When they could no longer stand it, the faculty and staff appointed mild-mannered elementary speech therapist Tanya Barnes to speak to Principal Thomas on their behalf.

"You talk too long," she said to the bathroom mirror. *True*, she thought, *but too abrupt.* "Lord, give me the words," she prayed as she prepared to deliver her message.

"May I talk with you?" she began as the principal answered her knock on his office door. Closing his door, she gently explained the thoughts of her co-workers. Upon reflection, Principal Thomas agreed and thanked her for speaking up—and for doing so professionally and with kindness.

Are you faced with a situation where you must speak the truth? Ask God to help you do it in a loving manner.

RESPECT DOESN'T ALWAYS LOOK LIKE AGREEMENT, BUT IT IS ALWAYS INFORMED BY LOVE.

*"I have called you by your name; You are Mine."*

**ISAIAH 43:1 NKJV**

---

*Never forget to be truthful and kind. Hold these virtues tightly. Write them deep within your heart. If you want favor with both God and man, and a reputation for good judgment and common sense, then trust the Lord completely; don't ever trust yourself. In everything you do, put God first, and he will direct you and crown your efforts with success.*

**PROVERBS 3:3-6 TLB**

---

*By thy favor, O Lord, thou hadst established me as a strong mountain.*

**PSALM 30:7 RSV**

# ENCOURAGED

Ms. Mason looked at Titus slumped in the back row of the classroom. He stared at the clock. Ms. Mason knew Titus hated school — well, not completely. He didn't mind the work, and he responded well to all his teachers. For Titus, school wouldn't be bad at all if it weren't for the other students.

She had noticed that Titus was often called names by a couple of troublemakers, but he seemed to hate being ignored by everyone else even more. In a previous conversation Ms. Mason had shared, "I know it hurts, Titus," and she shared a story from her own high school days. It may not seem like much comfort now, but you are important to God. He knows your name."

A few days later, as Ms. Mason passed out the graded test papers, Titus turned toward her encouraging voice . . . and Titus aced this test. Nice work." *For that brief moment, everyone knew his name*, Ms. Mason thought. *And I believe he'll soon realize that God has known it all along.*

You can be sure that God knows your name as well.

---

**GOD DOESN'T FORGET NAMES—THEY'RE WRITTEN IN PERMANENT INK ON HIS HEART.**

*I lift my eyes to the hills—where does my help come from? My help comes from the Lord, the Maker of heaven and earth.*

**PSALMS 121:1-2**

*It is God who arms me with strength, and makes my way perfect.*

**PSALM 18:32 NKJV**

*Finally, my brethren, be strong in the Lord and in the power of His might. Put on the whole armor of God, that you may be able to stand against the wiles of the devil.*

**EPHESIANS 6:10-11 NKJV**

# LOOKING FOR WORDS

Sarah felt like running—not a very adult thing to do. Besides, what was so horrible about confronting Rhonda, a fellow teacher? "I need to talk to you," Sarah had said on the phone, hoping her tone was friendly, not ominous. Rhonda had agreed.

"Get some help—" too confrontational. "I really care about you, Rhonda, but you're messing up big time—" still too harsh. "I can't be your friend if you keep—" ugh! There was no pretty way to say it. "Dear God, I have no clue how to talk to her," Sarah prayed. "Please give me the right words to say." Just then Rhonda walked into the room with a smile Sarah knew would soon be gone. The tears flowed, but so did the words—the right words. Sarah could hear them come from her mouth, and she knew they were God's by the wonderful kindness in them.

Do you need to speak truthful words to rescue a friend? God is eager and willing to help you.

WISDOM IS SEEING LIFE FROM GOD'S PERSPECTIVE.

*A sweet friendship refreshes the soul.*

**PROVERBS 27:9 MSG**

---

*A friend loves at all times, and a brother is born for adversity*

**PROVERBS 17:17 NKJV**

---

*Greater love has no one than this, than to lay down one's life for his friends.*

**JOHN 15:13 NKJV**

# HANDS OF LOVE

Nan finished setting the table and sat down. Immediately, she thought of Jeff. Mostly she thought of his hands. They were strong hands, to be certain. He'd helped her rearrange the furniture in her first grade classroom three times. He understood that she wanted things perfect for her new students that first day.

They were gentle hands too. Hands that surrounded Nan with a hug after her mother died. Hands that prepared and brought her a meal when she was recovering from surgery. And they were capable hands. Hands that fixed a broken pipe in the middle of the night and played beautiful music on the piano.

A knock on the door woke Nan from her daydream. She walked over and peeked through the peephole. She laughed aloud at the distorted image of Jeff's hands covering his face. Nan smiled. *Those are the hands of a true friend,* she thought. And suddenly realized, *Those are the hands of God too!*

Take time today to thank God for the true friends He's placed in your life. They are a glimpse of His love to you.

> **TRUE FRIENDSHIP IS ONE OF GOD'S MOST PRECIOUS GIFTS.**

*Make yourselves at home in my love.*

**JOHN 15:9 MSG**

---

*The Lord is good, a refuge in times of trouble. He cares for those who trust in Him.*

**NAHUM 1:7**

---

*We have known and believed the love that God hath to us. God is love; and he that dwelleth in love dwelleth in God, and God in him.*

**1 JOHN 4:16 KJV**

# CUSHIONED

Try this little experiment. Get your favorite drink — a cup of coffee, hot chocolate, or maybe a glass of cold milk. Now, choose a favorite snack. Maybe it's time to open that box of cookies you've been eyeing. Ready? Okay, now find the most comfortable place in your house. Or perhaps your favorite place isn't in your house at all. Go there now.

Are you comfortable? Breathe deeply. Sip your drink. Nibble on your snack. Close your eyes if you like. Daydream about wonderful things — bike rides along a cool stream; fragrant, warm breezes after a summer rain; snowflakes drifting past the window.

Are you feeling warm? Safe? At home? That's how God wants you to feel in His love. Though the world swirls around you and often drags you into its maelstrom, God's love is always near. Soak it in. Drench yourself in it. Learn its familiar and comforting rhythms and visit often.

> GOD'S LOVE IS A PLACE YOU CAN ALWAYS CALL HOME.

*You have freed me from my chains.*

**PSALM 116:16**

---

*The Lord knows how to save those who serve him when troubles come.*

**2 PETER 2:9 NCV**

---

*My eyes are always looking to the Lord for help, for he alone can rescue me from the traps of my enemies. May integrity and honesty protect me, for I put my hope in You.*

**PSALMS 25:15, 21 NLT**

# BONDAGE BREAKERS

Tony's arrest stunned the faculty, student body, and parents. How could someone they thought they knew be addicted to pornography? As Peter listened from the third row of the auditorium, he stared uncomfortably at his own shoes and thought, *How soon until someone discovers my secret, as well?*

It was those e-mails he kept receiving. The ones marked XXX. At first he'd opened one by mistake. As for the rest, well, he rationalized that just looking really didn't hurt anything. But it sure seemed to have hurt Tony. *Lord, help me*, he prayed to himself. *I don't know what to do to stop.* That moment he felt God heard Him.

The first step to battling any addiction is admitting there's a battle. Is there any area in your life that is increasingly out of your control? Ask God for help, but don't stop there. Confess what you're doing to a trusted friend or counselor who'll hold you accountable. Get the help you need, even if it's difficult or embarrassing. It's a battle worth winning.

WE CANNOT SAY NO TO TEMPTATION WITHOUT SAYING YES TO SOMETHING FAR BETTER.

*"My chosen ones will have satisfaction in their work."*

**ISAIAH 65:22 MSG**

---

*People may make plans in their minds, but the Lord decides what they will do.*

**PROVERBS 16:9 NCV**

---

*O Lord, you are my light! You make my darkness bright.*

**2 SAMUEL 22:29 TLB**

# IS YOUR CAREER IN GEAR?

The proper wrench turns a bolt with ease. When cutting grass, a lawn mower is preferable to pinking shears. Fins work better than heels when snorkeling. Fishermen prefer poles over slingshots if they're serious about catching their limit. Obvious, right?

Then doesn't it make sense that you'll function most effectively if you work in areas that maximize the way God's designed you? It's like using the right tool for the job.

Do you really know what you're best at? It may not be what your parents always pushed you to be or what pays the highest salary (Gifted teachers know that, for sure!). But doing it will allow you to be the person God has created you to be. Are you where God wants you to be in your profession? Talk to God about it.

Ignoring what makes you unique can make life as uncomfortable as wearing the wrong size shoes.

HOWEVER FAR YOU GO, IT IS NOT MUCH USE IF IT IS NOT IN THE RIGHT DIRECTION.

*I have hidden your word in my heart.*

**PSALM 119:11**

---

*I have written to you, children, because you have known the Father. I have written to you who are mature because you know Christ, the One who is from the beginning. I have written to you who are young because you are strong with God's word living in your hearts, and you have won your battle with Satan.*

**1 JOHN 2:14 NLT**

---

*We are not, like so many, peddler's of God's word; but as men of sincerity, as commissioned by God, in the sight of God we speak in Christ.*

**2 CORINTHIANS 2:17 RSV**

# AFLOAT

Were it not for the fact that he was drifting farther and farther into the middle of the lake, Jerry might have been enchanted by this moment. What could be a better way to spend his spring break than a perfect foggy morning of fishing on a beautiful lake? But there was this little problem: he was out of gas — without oars.

In a few hours, the lake would be teeming with life above the waterline. Someone will see me, he reasoned. Still Jerry couldn't seem to get rid of the knot in the pit of his stomach. How could he chase the anxiety away and enjoy his morning retreat?

Then Jerry had an idea. *I wonder how many scripture passages I can quote by heart,* he wondered. Not many, but the ones he knew made him aware of God's comforting presence in the boat. Two hours later, he heard the familiar sound of an outboard motor. As he hooked up the tow rope, Jerry decided he needed to do two things right away: stock his boat with oars and learn more scripture.

SCRIPTURE IS FAR HIGHER AND WIDER THAN OUR NEED.

*You have turned for me my mourning into dancing.*

**PSALM 30:11 NKJV**

---

*One final word, friends. We ask you— urge is more like it—that you keep on doing what we told you to do to please God, not in a dogged religious plod, but in a living, spirited dance.*

**1 THESSALONIANS 4:1 MSG**

---

*"You shall go out in joy, and be led forth in peace; the mountains and the hills before you shall break forth into singing, and all the trees of the field shall clap their hands."*

**ISAIAH 55:12 RSV**

# GET ON YOUR FEET

It was time for the church offering—not a modern dance recital. But the music lilted Twila's heart so suddenly, she felt as if it could lift her out of her seat as well. Wouldn't Mrs. Martinson, sitting next to her, have a "conniption?" Twila smiled at the picture that came to mind and decided she'd wait until she got home. Then she would turn up the music and dance—with God. In times of dance, she felt Him close by.

Just as our words communicate with God, so do our actions. Some people kneel in adoration; some raise their hands in praise; some dance as a way of expressing emotions too deep for words. Dancing often conveys feelings of joy at celebrations. But dance can express countless emotions, including awe, happiness, sorrow, and even anger. God understands the language of the heart, no matter how it's expressed.

If music moves you, put on a song that draws you to God, and see where your feet take you.

THE WORSHIP OF GOD IS NOT A RULE OF SAFETY—IT IS AN ADVENTURE OF THE SPIRIT.

*I want you woven into a tapestry of love, in touch with everything there is to know of God.*

**COLOSSIANS 2:2 MSG**

---

*The meek shall obtain fresh joy in the Lord, and the poor among men shall exult in the Holy One of Israel.*

**ISAIAH 29:19 RSV**

---

*Those who have reason to be thankful should continually be singing praises to the Lord.*

**JAMES 5:13 TLB**

# SOAKING IN IT

"I get it! I finally get it!" Sandy shouted as she ran around the table and embraced her teacher and tutor, Karen. Truly it was a wonderful moment for student and teacher. Karen had tutored Sandy in algebra for a whole semester. But it was only after Sandy realized that God wanted to have a personal relationship with her that her mind opened up to a real understanding of mathematics. Karen laughed as she watched Sandy — she could barely contain herself.

"I want to learn everything," Sandy said, looking directly into Karen's eyes. "I want to soak up all there is to know. Will you help me?" Tears mingled with giggles as she settled back into her chair at Karen's kitchen table.

"I will, Sandy. As long as you help me," answered Karen.

"Me help you —?" Sandy smiled quizzically. "But how? I don't know anything."

"It's not what you know," said Karen. "It's your excitement. I want to feel that again. We can help each other. Deal?"

"It's a deal!"

Is your relationship with God lacking excitement? If so, share it with someone. The flame will burn again.

---

**IT IS A BAD THING TO BE SATISFIED SPIRITUALLY.**

*"I'd sell off the whole world to get you back, trade the creation just for you."*

**ISAIAH 43:4 MSG**

---

*God so loved the world that He gave his only Son, that whoever believes in Him should not perish but have eternal life.*

**JOHN 3:16 RSV**

---

*We know that we have passed from death unto life, because we love the brethren.*

**1 JOHN 3:14 KJV**

# LOVE STORY

It had all the makings of a great action film—some guy sacrificing his own life to save his true love. Kara loved stories like that, but they always left her feeling inexplicably sad and empty. *If only there was someone who would rescue me,* she usually thought.

But this time, the story she was hearing wasn't fiction. It was coming from a church pulpit. When Kara joined her friend Carl for his church's Easter service, she had expected to hear what a horrible person she was—that she had let God down and had better get her life together. Instead, she heard that Someone came to earth to rescue her. She heard that there really was a Hero who loved her. Kara knew she'd finally found what her heart had always longed for. At that moment she felt that God had heard the cry of her heart.

Do you long for a love that is true and lasting? God has already given His life for you, and He is waiting to claim you for His own.

> IT IS NOT YOUR HOLD ON CHRIST THAT SAVES YOU, BUT HIS HOLD ON YOU!

*He who refreshes others will himself
be refreshed.*

**PROVERBS 11:25**

---

*Rejoice with those who rejoice; and
weep with those who weep.*

**ROMANS 12:15 NKJV**

---

*If we walk in the light, as he is in the light,
we have fellowship one with another.*

**1 JOHN 1:7 KJV**

# REACHING OUT

After Jean's husband died, life never really felt like it was back to "normal." Time lessened the pain, but there was a weariness that filled her heart. She just couldn't seem to shake it.

One Saturday afternoon, Jean agreed to help a friend at a riding stable. The stable was known for its therapeutic riding program for kids with physical and emotional problems. All Jean did was help kids get on and off horses all day. She shared both laughter and frustration with the kids, but most of all, she shared their sense of accomplishment and hope. When she arrived home, Jean realized something had changed in her heart, and she knew just who to thank for it.

God created us to live in community. Reaching outside of your own pain to help others in the midst of theirs may be just what God uses to refresh your weary soul. Find a way to be a source of refreshment for someone else.

> GRIEF CAN BE YOUR SERVANT, HELPING YOU TO FEEL MORE COMPASSION FOR OTHERS WHO HURT.

*He satisfies the longing soul, and fills the hungry soul with goodness.*

**PSALM 107:9 NKJV**

---

*I pray that the God who gives hope will fill you with much joy and peace while you trust in him. Then your hope will overflow by the power of the Holy Spirit.*

**ROMANS 15:13 NCV**

---

*Lord, you alone are my hope; I've trusted you from childhood.*

**PSALM 71:5 TLB**

# FULL

"What do you long for?" The small-group leader had posed this same question twelve weeks earlier. Back then Terry had known exactly what to say. "I long for a job I love, a chance to play my music, and a good night's sleep." Others had offered similar responses. But now, after all they'd studied and explored together, the answer wasn't so simple.

"I'm not quite sure what I long for," Terry began. "Perhaps it's a chance to know God more intimately." Others nodded, then added their insights. One thing was certain—he knew what longing was now. Those things he'd mentioned twelve weeks ago? Sure, he still dreamed of them, but his longing was for something deeper.

Your deepest longings are placed within you by God. They cannot be filled by a better job, more time for your hobbies, or a good night's sleep. Only the Creator of the longing can truly fill it.

GOD IS NEVER FOUND ACCIDENTALLY.

*"I will grant peace in the land, and you will lie down and no one will make you afraid."*

**LEVITICUS 26:6**

---

*Save me, O God, because I have come to you for refuge. I said to Him, "You are my Lord; I have no other help but yours."*

**PSALM 16:1-2 TLB**

---

*The Lord is my light and my salvation; whom shall I fear? the Lord is the strength of my life; of whom shall I be afraid?*

**PSALM 27:1 NKJV**

# BATTLE ZONE

The lion will lie down with the lamb. *Right. And Drake will apologize, tell his thugs to back off, and become my best student,* Will thought sarcastically. He wondered if he should wait a few more minutes before leaving the safety of the school building. Maybe Drake would give up and go home.

No such luck. There they were, standing at the end of the path, staring his way. "Okay—okay—this is the part where you guys beat me up," Will called out. "I know how it goes. Just get it over with, okay?"

Will felt like a lamb ready for the slaughter as Drake and his friends approached. "Beat you up? Nah. Me and my buddies are actually kinda sorry about all that stuff," Drake said. Will waited for the punch line—or the punch. Neither came.

"My coach said it's my own fault I failed your class," Drake said. As the boys walked away, Will paused to thank God for turning a lion's roar into a soft purr.

> WHEN WE HAVE NOTHING LEFT BUT GOD, THEN WE BECOME AWARE THAT GOD IS ENOUGH.

*"I carried you on eagles' wings and brought you to myself."*

**EXODUS 19:4**

---

*You will find Him if you seek Him with all your heart.*

**DEUTERONOMY 4:29 NKJV**

---

*As for me, how good it is to be near God!*

**PSALM 73:28 NLT**

# CAN'T GET THERE ALONE

When was the last time you were too tired to move? After a day at school filled with rowdy students and tons of papers to grade? When you finally finished moving that firewood from the driveway to the backyard? When you clicked off the kids' bedroom lights and settled into your easy chair after a day as child chauffeur and homework helper?

It's not unusual to feel too exhausted by life to seek an audience with God. That's when the prayers sound something like this: "Lord. I'll get to that quiet time right after this nap—zzzz."

There's nothing wrong with rest. Even Jesus went away to rest when He had a tough day. But you also need time with God. Ask the God who first took you to Him to take you to Him once again. You'll find just enough energy to leap into His arms.

> FIRST GOD TAKES YOU TO HIM, THEN HE
> BRINGS HIMSELF TO YOU.

*He will be the sure foundation for your times, a rich store of salvation and wisdom and knowledge; the fear of the Lord is the key to this treasure.*

**ISAIAH 33:6**

---

*Yes, if you want better insight and discernment, and are searching for them as you would for lost money or hidden treasure, then wisdom will be given you, and knowledge of God himself; you will soon learn the importance of reverence for the Lord and of trusting him.*

**PROVERBS 2:3-5 TLB**

---

*The Lord by wisdom founded the earth; by understanding He established the heavens.*

**PROVERBS 3:19 NKJV**

# WISE UP

**K**yle was a card-carrying Mensa member—and proud of it. To Kyle and his parents, anything less than straight A's was unthinkable, any degree less than a Ph.D., unacceptable. "Average" was not a word Kyle could relate to. He grew up believing he was a step above the ordinary, which made it easy to look down on those around him.

Then a friend, whose IQ happened to be even higher than his own, introduced Kyle to a God who valued wisdom over intelligence and compassion over knowledge. That moment turned Kyle's world upside down because he discovered he was no longer on top. But, at the same time, he'd never felt more valued or more challenged by the mysteries of life that lay before him.

Intelligence and faith are not only compatible but also complementary. What do you do with what you learn about God? Is your spiritual life more like an intellectual exercise or a growing relationship?

KNOWLEDGE IS HORIZONTAL. WISDOM IS VERTICAL—IT COMES DOWN FROM ABOVE.

*Your path led through the sea, your way through the mighty waters, though your footprints were not seen.*

**PSALM 77:19**

---

*Faith comes by hearing, and hearing by the word of God.*

**ROMANS 10:17 NKJV**

---

*"The just shall live by his faith."*

**HABAKKUK 2:4 NKJV**

# RISING TIDES

Half buried in a small pile of rocks sat the perfect shell, its spiral silhouette unbroken by the pounding surf. Jasmine picked it up and dusted off the sticky grains of sand. Although she walked this beach every morning, a shell like this was a rare find. The shore was littered with bits of shell, coral, and smoothly sanded glass, but the rocks and the ferocity of the sea deposited most of its treasures here in pieces.

*What a journey this shell must have had,* Jasmine thought. She couldn't help but think of her own rocky journey over the past few years. She could finally look back on it all and see how God had brought her through, unbroken. Jasmine put the shell in her pocket, a reminder of God's faithfulness through the storms of life.

What can you do to remember God's faithfulness when you can't see Him clearly during difficult times?

WHEN OUTWARD STRENGTH IS BROKEN, FAITH RESTS ON THE PROMISES.

*You are my hiding place; you will protect me from trouble.*

**PSALM 32:7**

---

*God guards you from every evil, He guards your very life. He guards you when you leave and when you return, He guards you now, He guards you always.*

**PSALM 121:7-8 MSG**

---

*The name of the Lord is a strong fortress the godly run to Him and are safe.*

**PROVERBS 18:10 NLT**

# PARENTAL PERSPECTIVE

"**N**o, Joey! Put it down!" Colleen yelled at her two-year-old son from across the kitchen. Surprised by the tone of his mother's voice, Joey immediately dropped the knife on the floor and began to cry. Colleen tenderly picked up the tow-headed toddler and held him. tightly in her arms. She must have left the knife on the table after cutting his apple for lunch. "A knife is not a toy!" she tried to explain, feeling a mixture of guilt and relief.

*He's just too little to understand,* she thought. *I guess sometimes "because I said so" is the only answer I can really give.* Colleen suddenly thought of God as her Parent and realized, *I guess that's also the only answer God can give sometimes too.*

Just like toddlers reaching for a shiny knife, God's children often ignorantly reach for, or pray for, things that could harm them. Remember that when God answers, even His no's, are always motivated by love.

> OUR GOD DOES NOT ALWAYS ANSWER OUR PRAYERS AS WE REQUEST. BUT HE DOES FOR US, AS FOR OUR LORD IN THE GARDEN; HE STRENGTHENS US.

*"Fear not, for I am with you; Be not dismayed, for I am your God. I will strengthen you, Yes, I will help you, I will uphold you with My righteous right hand."*

**ISAIAH 41:10 NKJV**

---

*Do not be anxious about anything, but in everything, by prayer and petition, with thanksgiving, present your requests to God. And the peace of God, which transcends all understanding, will guard your hearts and your minds in Christ Jesus.*

**PHILIPPIANS 4:6-7**

---

*"For I, the Lord your God, hold your right hand; it is I who say to you. 'Fear not, I will help you.'"*

**ISAIAH 41:13 RSV**

# HIS TURN

Jill sat in the teachers' lounge at Harris Middle School. It was only fourth period, yet she felt as though she had endured an entire day of classes. Mornings with three classes of more than thirty thirteen- and fourteen-year-olds in each class seemed to suck every ounce of strength from her.

If one student defied her authority, the entire period became a battle zone, and Jill was tired of standing her ground. Jill prayed, They're so strong-willed and determined to control my classroom. Why won't they listen? Why aren't they hungry to learn? I can't do this, Lord. It's Your turn.

Immediately a new strength filled Jill's heart. Perhaps that is what God had been waiting for—His turn. Jill realized it was time to let go and give God control of her classroom. I give it all to You.

When Jill stepped into the classroom, the students were unusually quiet. They seemed attentive and perhaps just out of fuel. Jill silently thanked God. She could see a change in her classroom—and on her students' faces.

GIVE GOD HIS TURN.

*From the fullness of his grace we have all received one blessing after another.*

**JOHN 1:16**

---

*You know that the lord has chosen for himself those who are loyal to him. The lord listens when I pray to him.*

**PSALM 4:3 NCV**

---

*Oh, give thanks to the Lord, for He is good! For His mercy endures forever.*

**1 CHRONICLES 16:34 NKJV**

# AMAZING GRACE

"Bless us, O Lord, for these Thy gifts which we are about to receive." As a little girl, Grace had always loved that prayer. She'd secretly believed it was named after her, or she after it. She was never quite sure which. But as an adult, Grace felt that praying before meals was nothing more than a well-intentioned tradition—until Jeff and his family came to dinner.

As they sat down at the table, Jeff asked her if he could say the blessing. "Of course," she said politely and bowed her head. But his words took her by surprise. He sounded truly grateful, speaking from the heart. From that day on, Grace—both the woman and the prayer before meals—was never the same.

When you thank God for His blessings in your life, is it more like a thank-you card your parents have forced you to write or a love letter from your heart?

---

**PRAYER REQUIRES MORE OF THE HEART THAN OF THE TONGUE.**

*The Lord your God is with you, he is mighty to save.*

**ZEPHANIAH 3:17**

---

*He does not fear bad news, nor live in dread of what may happen. For he is settled in his mind that Jehovah will take care of him.*

**PSALM 112:7 TLB**

---

*"Don't be afraid. I am with you. Don't tremble with fear. I am your God. I will make you strong, as I protect you with my arm and give you victories."*

**ISAIAH 41:10 CEV**

# CLOSE CALL

Rushing to get to her classroom on time, out of the corner of her eye, Gail saw the blur of a red truck. In a split second, she realized it was going to run the light. As the words, "God, no!" escaped from her lips, everything seemed to go into slow motion—Gail hitting the brakes; her car straining to stop; and the truck swerving, missing her by inches, then speeding down the road as if nothing had happened. Her heart still racing, she pulled over to the curb to catch her breath.

While her adrenaline still seemed to be bracing for the worst, Gail found herself rejoicing in the best—the fact that she was alive and unhurt. It was a blessing she'd taken for granted just moments before, and now she was filled with a renewed appreciation for how precious life was—and how fragile. As she resumed her commute, her heart couldn't stop giving thanks.

How has God's protection touched your life today?

BEING PRAYERFUL IS AS IMPORTANT AS BEING CAREFUL.

*Say to those with fearful hearts, "Be strong, do not fear; your God will come."*

**ISAIAH 35:4**

---

*Be of good courage, and He shall strengthen your heart, all you who hope in the Lord.*

**PSALM 31:24 KJV**

---

*I sought the Lord, and he answered me, and delivered me from all my fears.*

**PSALM 34:4 RSV**

# TEST OF COURAGE

When the nurse mentioned, an MRI, Gloria began to panic. It wasn't the results of the test she was afraid of; it was the thought of being shoved into that little tube. Small spaces had always terrified her. As a kid, she couldn't even play hide-and-seek without fearing her wildly beating heart would give her away. She knew it was irrational, but that didn't make her fear any less real.

As the test began, Gloria closed her eyes and pictured God at her side, holding her hand and making sure there was enough air for her to breathe. Then she began to pray for all of the friends she knew were praying for her. She began to sing praise songs in her mind, and she repeated the Twenty-Third Psalm. In those God-filled moments, her anxiety was soon replaced with peace.

If you're facing a frightening situation in your life, keep your mind on God. He'll see you through.

ONLY HE WHO CAN SAY, "THE LORD IS MY STRENGTH," CAN SAY, "OF WHOM SHALL I BE AFRAID?"

*Weeping may remain for a night, but rejoicing comes in the morning.*

**PSALM 30:5**

---

*Yes, I will bless the Lord and not forget the glorious things he does for me. He forgives all my sins. He heals me.*

**PSALM 103:2-3 TLB**

---

*All the crowd sought to touch him, for power came forth from him and healed them all.*

**LUKE 6:19 RSV**

# HOPE FOR HEALING

When Phil got out of bed, he realized something was missing. He bent over and twisted to the right. The pain wasn't there anymore. After his back surgery, he had debated which was worse—the ailment or the cure. But today he found himself whistling as he hurried down to breakfast, thanking God for a day without excruciating pain.

That pain had made even the brightest day feel like the dead of night. There were times when he thought he couldn't stand it anymore—when it hurt to stand up and it hurt to lie down. Some nights seemed as if they would last forever. The only relief he found was in those moments of prayer when he felt, really felt, God's assurance that someday the pain would end. When it didn't happen overnight, he almost lost hope. But finally that morning came, and the pain was gone for good.

If you are in pain today, God can see you through it.

GOD DRIES TEARS FROM THE INSIDE OUT.

*We know that all things work together for good to those who love God.*

**ROMANS 8:28 NKJV**

---

*To the man who pleases him God gives wisdom and knowledge and joy.*

**ECCLESIASTES 2:26 RSV**

---

*Rejoice in the Lord always. I will say it again: Rejoice!*

**PHILIPPIANS 4:4**

# LIFE SUPREME

"What do you want on your pizza?" Jerri asked her class after they'd achieved their nine weeks goal and won the pizza contest.

"Everything!" a couple of teens said.

"Just cheese on mine," said another girl.

"Pepperoni!" several others cried.

Jerri laughed and clarified their order, "Okay, one pepperoni, one cheese, and one with everything. Even anchovies?"

"No way!" they shouted.

"Didn't think so," Jerri said. "How about some wood glue with that mozzarella? A pair of pantyhose alongside the pepperoni?" The kids all laughed. "You mean you don't want *everything* on your pizza?" she asked.

God says He'll work everything together for good in our lives. That means everything—anchovies, cod liver oil, all of it. But most of us want to pick off toppings we don't like. No one promised that life would "taste" great all the time. But somehow God can turn even the most unpalatable situations into a gourmet feast.

WHEN IT COMES TO PROMISES, GOD
DELIVERS!

*[Love] always protects, always trusts, always hopes, always perseveres.*

**1 CORINTHIANS 13:7**

---

*His lord said to him, "Well done, good and faithful servant; you were faithful over a few things, I will make you ruler over many things. Enter into the joy of your lord."*

**MATTHEW 25:21 NKJV**

---

*Do you see a man skillful in his work? He will stand before kings; he will not stand before obscure men.*

**PROVERBS 22:29 RSV**

# LIVING FOR
# THE LONG RUN

Working with the drama club group energized Corey — most of the time. He liked for the kids to see him in a role other than coach. But the dark clouds that were on the horizon this morning were now directly overhead. All he wanted to do was stay home and watch the football game on TV, but he knew the threat of a downpour would make the scavenger hunt all the more exciting in the kids' eyes.

When he arrived, the rain had already started to fall. A teen from the group ran up to him with an umbrella. "I'm so glad you came, Coach Johnson," Clay said. "Remember that talk we had last week about prayer? Could I ask you a couple of questions?" Corey couldn't help but smile. He knew the time he spent today was much more important than any football score.

Corey wasn't motivated by a desire to receive recognition for his efforts; he was interested in making an eternal difference in the lives of others. What motivates you?

WHY NOT INVEST JOUR LIFE IN SOMETHING
THAT GIVES ETERNAL RETURNS?

*Give thanks in all circumstances.*

**1 THESSALONIANS 5:18**

---

*In everything you do, stay away from complaining and arguing, so that no one can speak a word of blame against you. You are to live clean, innocent lives as children of God in a dark world full of crooked and perverse people. Let your lives shine brightly before them.*

**PHILIPPIANS 2:14-15 NLT**

---

*"Here I am! I stand at the door and knock. If you hear my voice and open the door, I will come in and eat with you, and you will eat with me."*

**REVELATION 3:20 NCV**

# AN ATTITUDE OF GRATITUDE

Cleaning toilets wasn't Dawn's idea of a great way to spend Friday night, but somebody had to do it. As she began rinsing the sink, she caught sight of herself in the bathroom mirror—no makeup, her sweatshirt sleeves pushed up over her elbows, and a stray strand of hair escaping from her ponytail. *It's a good thing I'm not expecting company,* she thought.

Actually, that's what Dawn wanted most. She dreaded another weekend with no one to talk to. Then it was almost as though she could hear God say, *How about talking to Me?*

"Okay, so what do we have to talk about?" she answered back.

Moments from her day came quickly to her mind—reasons for thanksgiving she'd almost overlooked. His love for her flooded her heart. She even thanked God that she had a bathroom to clean, instead of an outhouse.

When you need someone to talk to, God is always there to keep you company.

GOD CAN NO MORE DO WITHOUT US THAN WE CAN DO WITHOUT HIM.

*All you have made will praise you, O Lord.*

**PSALM 145:10**

---

*O give thanks to the Lord, for he is good; his steadfast love endures for ever!*

**PSALM 107:1 RSV**

---

*We thank God! He gives us the victory through our Lord Jesus Christ.*

**1 CORINTHIANS 15:57 NCV**

# A MOUNTAIN, A HAWK, AND PRAISE

The last hundred yards made up for the previous half-mile of shifting rocks and shirt-snagging underbrush. It was almost as if the mountain had admitted defeat and offered up an easy path to Cindy and Brian. They wove their way to a large, flat boulder and climbed onto it.

"Wow! Look at that!" Brian exclaimed. The treetops below swayed gently in the breeze. A hawk soared gracefully overhead. Tiny mountain flowers smiled in the sunshine. The rhythm of this natural world was unfamiliar to two first-year city teachers weaned on computers and television.

Cindy spun slowly to soak up as much as possible. "It's as if all of nature is singing out to the Creator," she said in awe. Time passed much too quickly, and as they climbed down the rocky path, they were silent. They didn't want to interrupt the most excellent praise and worship service they'd ever experienced.

God created this huge, wonderful world just to impress you. Be sure and thank Him for it.

IF YOU WANT TO KNOW WHAT PRAISE LOOKS LIKE, STUDY A BIRD IN FLIGHT, A FLOWER IN BLOOM, OR THE PURPLE-HUED SILHOUETTE OF A MOUNTAIN RANGE.

*Love forgets mistakes.*

**PROVERBS 17:9 TLB**

---

*A good name is to be chosen rather than great riches, loving favor rather than silver and gold.*

**PROVERBS 22:1 NKJV**

---

*"Blessed are the merciful: for they shall obtain mercy."*

**MATTHEW 5:7 KJV**

# OVERLOOKED

As the pastor read off the Sunday school teachers' names, the volunteers rose to their feet to the sound of applause. But Terry remained in her seat, her eyes on her shoes and color rising in her cheeks. She'd taught the singles' class for the last two years, but for some reason, her name wasn't on the list. She knew it was just a mistake—a typing error—but it still hurt.

After the service, Terry decided to make a hasty retreat, but one of her students called out to her. The woman gave her a quick hug and said warmly, "I noticed they forgot to mention your name this morning. I just wanted to tell you how much your class has meant to me. Thanks for everything." Right then Terry knew that God understood, how much the oversight had mattered to her.

Mistakes do happen, but you can be sure God sees them and their effect on you. Trust Him to care, and leave those events in His hands.

DON'T LET AN OFFENSE BUILD A RELATIONAL FENCE.

*Don't put your life in the hands of experts who know nothing of life, of salvation life.*

**PSALM 146:3 MSG**

*There are many devices in a man's heart; nevertheless the counsel of the Lord, that shall stand.*

**PROVERBS 19:21 KJV**

*Guide me in your truth, and teach me, my God, my Savior. I trust you all day long.*

**PSALM 25:5 NCV**

# BAD ADVICE

It was some of the worst advice Jake had ever been given: "You have to try skydiving!" Hanging tight to the airplane seat, he now wished he hadn't said, "Why not?"

He contemplated other bad advice he'd listened to over the years. "Go for the money, become a doctor." "There's no money in teaching, even if it is your passion."

"Jake, your turn!" Wayne gestured as he yelled to his friend above the engine noise.

Remind me never to listen to you again," Jake called back, before stepping out of the plane. He tensed up when he felt a sudden jerk, but then he realized it was just the chute opening. A moment later he was able to relax while floating slowly toward the ground far below. At that moment, Jake thanked God for the other sudden "jerk" that had pulled him out of medical school, into the teaching field, and back to Him.

DON'T LISTEN TO ADVICE THAT DOESN'T HAVE ITS FOUNDATION BOLTED TO GOD'S WORD.

*If the Lord delights in a man's way, He makes his steps firm.*

**PSALM 37:23**

---

*I lead in the way of righteousness, in the midst of the paths of judgment: that I may cause those that love me to inherit substance; and I will fill their treasures.*

**PROVERBS 8:20-21 KJV**

---

*The way of the righteous is like the first gleam of dawn, which shines ever brighter until the full light of day.*

**PROVERBS 4:18 NLT**

# THE PERFECT PART

As the curtain went down, the parents' applause filled the auditorium. Emily was good-naturedly pushed out onto the stage to receive a bouquet of flowers and words of thanks for her work in putting together the production. Although she was much more comfortable behind the curtain than in front of it, she also had a few words of thanks to give. She thanked God for the courage to take on something bigger than she could pull off on her own.

Emily had always pictured a leader as someone filled with confidence and authority—someone gruff and tough. Her personality was just the opposite. But when she was asked to direct the first school performance this year as a first-year teacher, she had felt God's peace in saying yes. From there on out, she had seen God take her common talents and use them in remarkable ways.

Are you allowing God to use your talents for His glory? Are you willing to take some risks to let Him do that?

WITH GOD, HUMAN EFFORTS CAN HAVE DIVINE RESULTS.

*If you know the right thing to do and
don't do it, that, for you, is evil.*

**JAMES 4:17 MSG**

---

*Above all these things put on charity,
which is the bond of perfectness.*

**COLOSSIANS 3:14 KJV**

---

*The integrity of the upright guides them,
but the crookedness of the treacherous
destroys them.*

**PROVERBS 11:3 RSV**

# SILENCE ISN'T ALWAYS GOLDEN

Carol sat on the edge of the deck, feet dangling and head down. She'd just gotten the news that Jim had been suspended without pay. Soon she'd get a call from the superintendent or the school board, inviting her for an interview. They'd grill her about what she knew of Jim's habits in the classroom and on the field, and Carol would walk away feeling just as rotten as she felt now.

Carol wouldn't be implicated for what she knew. In fact, she had guessed wrong about what was going on. The clues led her to believe Jim was having an affair. Instead, her coworker paid off referees for wins during sporting events.

Carol mentally kicked herself for missing several opportunities to talk to him. Once Jim had said something cryptic about "a secret that was making him a happy man." Then just last week he had said, "I could be in a lot of trouble soon."

She felt Cod whisper, "It's not too late." She jumped up and headed for the phone. This time she would act on His holy nudge and talk to Jim.

The only way to help others is to listen for God's instruction and move out on it.

IF THE SILENCE IS DEAFENING, PERHAPS IT'S TIME TO BREAK IT.

*"Blessed are the pure in heart, for they will see God."*

**MATTHEW 5:8**

---

*Do not think you are better than you are. You must decide what you really are by the amount of faith God has given you.*

**ROMANS 12:3 NCV**

---

*You are all children of God through faith in Christ Jesus.*

**GALATIANS 3:27 NCV**

# OUT OF THE MOUTH
# OF BABES

Beverly thought she'd heard it all during her ten years as the director of the child development center. "Why is that woman so fat?" "Look at that man with the funny face!" There's a time in every child's life when unfiltered truth spills out freely, often creating rather embarrassing situations.

But in addition to the embarrassing moments, Beverly had also experienced the most, precious ones. "Look, teacher, God is painting pictures with the clouds!"

"God's love is kinda like my pillow—all soft, and it smells like home." "I know we can't hear bunnies talk, but I bet God can."

Jesus asks you to become like a little child so you can see God clearly. The more you fill up your life with routine and a daily wheelbarrow full of trouble, the cloudier your vision will become. But when you become like a child, you will find that birds sing "Awesome God"; watercolors drip off God's paintbrush, forming rainbows; and God goes bowling in the thunder.

YOU CAN SEE GOD BEST WHEN YOU LOOK
THROUGH A CHILD'S EYES.

*"Walk before me in integrity of heart."*

**1 KINGS 9:4**

---

*You desire honesty from the heart, so you can teach me to be wise in my inmost being.*

**PSALM 51:6 NLT**

---

*I know, my God, that you test men to see if they are good; for you enjoy good men.*

**1 CHRONICLES 29:17 TLB**

# MISSTEPS

Erin rolled over and stared at the clock for one last time before finally climbing out of bed. Another sleepless night. When am I going to stop this? she wondered. She could feel God there, knowing what He knew. She felt the pressure that made sleep impossible. Then groggily, she showered, dressed, and headed out the door to face her college students for another day.

"You look terrible," said Barb, who was never much for subtlety. "What's wrong?"

"I'm just not sleeping much, that's all." Erin knew that wasn't all, but she was embarrassed for her best friend to know the truth.

"Can we talk?" Barb responded with a look of concern Erin hadn't seen on her face before. "What's really going on?"

Erin swallowed hard. She was tired of living two lives. Maybe it was time to come clean. *Dear God*, she prayed silently, *I don't know if You're still listening, but if You are, please give me the strength to be truthful.* "Barb, I have a problem," she began.

God loves you enough to help you get back onto the right path.

---

**THE STEPS ON THE STAIRWAY TO INTEGRITY ARE TOO FAR APART FOR YOU TO REACH WITHOUT GOD'S ASSISTANCE.**

*Before you trust, you have to listen. But unless Christ's Word is preached, there's nothing to listen to.*

**ROMANS 10:17 MSG**

---

*"What do you mean, 'If I can'?" Jesus asked. "Anything is possible if a person believes."*

**MARK 9:23 NLT**

---

*It is by faith we understand that the whole world was made by God's command so what we see was made by something that cannot be seen.*

**HEBREWS 11:3 NCV**

# SO MANY VOICES

Ron was going to be here in the hospital awhile. "You'll make a full recovery," the doctor had said, "but it will take some time." After three books, Ron was tired of reading. Instead, he decided to think.

On Thursday morning, his thoughts landed on the topic of religion. As a philosophy instructor, he'd studied them all — Buddhism, Islam, Christianity, and all sorts of New Age ideas — yet he still felt lost and alone. He tried to spend Friday in prayer, but he just didn't know whom to pray to. *I just can't put a face on these religions,* he thought. Saturday, he was depressed.

Sunday brought a guest. "Hi, my name's Thom. I used to be a patient here. You need some company?" Ron wondered why a stranger wanted to spend time with him, and then it began to make sense. Thom was a Christian. His religion wasn't about rules or systems. It was about relationships. Suddenly Christianity had a face — it looked like Thom, and God looked like Jesus of Nazareth.

> IF YOU CAN'T SEE THE TRUTH, PERHAPS YOU SHOULD LISTEN FOR IT INSTEAD.

*There is a time for everything, and a season for every activity under heaven.*

**ECCLESIASTES 3:1**

---

*Teach us to make the most of our time, so that we may grow in wisdom.*

**PSALM 90:12 NLT**

---

*Cry out for insight and understanding . . . Then you will understand what is right, just, and fair, and you will know how to find the right course of action every time.*

**PROVERBS 2:3-9 NLT**

# A TIME TO UPROOT

"I don't want to go." Six-year-old Jessie dropped to the bare floor, crossed her legs, and folded her arms. The last of the boxes had been loaded on the moving truck.

Karen sat down next to her daughter. "Honey, we can't stay here. Another family is moving in. Remember, you met their little boy?"

Jessie started to cry. "I don't want him to have my room." "You know we have to move, Jessie. Daddy has a new job at a new school in Texas. Don't you think we should go with him?" Jessie's chin quivered. Karen hugged the little girl who had her father's blue eyes. "Sometimes we just have to do hard things."

Jessie sighed and asked. "Is this one of those times?"

"Yes, honey," her mother replied, feeling the rightness about this move that came from time spent asking God about it.

You may not understand why God has allowed certain circumstances in your life. But you can know that He is right there in the midst of them with you. Together, you can do anything, no matter how difficult it might seem.

FAITH MAKES ALL THINGS POSSIBLE . . .
LOVE MAKES ALL THINGS EASY.

*The Lord preserves the faithful.*

**PSALM 31:23 NKJV**

---

*Christ, who suffered for you, is your example. Follow in his steps . . . He did not retaliate when he was insulted. When he suffered, he did not threaten to get even. He left his case in the hands of God, who always judges fairly.*

**1 PETER 2:21,23 NLT**

---

*Many are the afflictions of the righteous; but the Lord delivers him out of them all.*

**PSALM 34:19 RSV**

# SAVED BY THE BELL

Ostracized for speaking the truth about her faith, Abby Gillian quickly became the target for troublemakers' taunts. Then the taunts turned violent. "Where's your God now?" an angry student mocked as he slammed her against the wall.

The bruises were still visible when she returned to school. Some kids who'd made fun of her before fell silent. No one had thought anyone would actually hurt her. Rumors spread quickly: "Jake tried to kill Miss Gillian." "What did she do to deserve that?" "Nothing."

Abby heard the whispers, too, and in time, the rumors — and the taunts — died down. In fact, she became something of a legend around the school halls. "I really admire you . . . you stand up for what you believe," students would say in hushed tones. Some even wanted to know how she did it. Gillian was happy to tell them about her God.

Are you willing to stand up for what you believe?

---

IT IS HUMAN TO STAND WITH THE CROWD. IT IS DIVINE TO STAND ALONE.

---

*The Lord God will help me; therefore shall I not be confounded: therefore have I set my face like a flint, and I know that I shall not be ashamed.*

**ISAIAH 50:7 KJV**

---

*Take courage! Do not let your hands be weak, for your work shall be rewarded.*

**2 CHRONICLES 15:7 RSV**

---

*Answer me when I pray to you, my God who does what is right. Make things easier for me when I am in trouble. Have mercy on me and hear my prayer.*

**PSALM 4:1 NCV**

# GYM CLASS

It was more terrifying than the deepest, darkest dungeon. It was more distasteful than a plateful of brussel sprouts. And it was listed on Terri's fall schedule: P.E. She knew it stood for "physical education," but she read it as "excruciating pain." Even with budget cuts, how could they force her to teach a class she knew nothing about?

The first day she went over her expectations for the class. There was no running and no showers, everyone had to dress out. "Bring gym clothes tomorrow. We're playing basketball," Terri said. *Not basketball!* she thought. *Anything but that!*

When Tuesday came, Terri had prayed, *Lord, show me how to do what I need to do.* Suddenly she had a God-idea—student-led instruction. *God, it looks like this is the semester I learn how to pray!*

The strangest things bring us to our knees, but God is always glad to hear from us.

COURAGE ISN'T THE ABSENCE OF FEAR . . . IT'S DISCOVERING THE PRESENCE OF GOD IN THE MIDDLE OF FEAR.

*Where there is no vision, the people perish.*

**PROVERBS 29:18 KJV**

---

*Call to me and I will answer you, and will tell you great and hidden things which you have not known.*

**JEREMIAH 33:3 RSV**

---

*He reveals deep and mysterious things and knows what lies hidden in darkness, though he himself is surrounded by light.*

**DANIEL 2:22 NLT**

# BEYOND THE STARS

"Don't you wish you could go there?" asked Kellie, who was lying in the grass next to her sister. A warm wind rustled their hair in perfect unison, and they heard their children scampering around the blanket they were lying on.

"To the stars?" Jessica asked. "I don't think so."

"But it's incredible . . . it's so vast. Don't you want to know if there's anybody but us out there?"

Jessica rolled over, rested her chin on her elbows, and asked, "Why do you always ask these impossible questions? You sound like one of my students."

"It helps put everything else in perspective," Kellie said. "It's good to think big thoughts."

"No," her sister replied, "it hurts to think big thoughts. I prefer to ride whatever wave comes my way."

Kellie looked over at her sister. "Don't you have any dreams, Jess? Any pictures in your head that keep you motivated to grow and learn?" It was a hard question. Secretly, Jessica longed to have big dreams. She longed to see further. Father, she prayed silently, give me a dream too—one that will help other people.

> GOD PAINTS VISION INTO THE HEARTS OF THOSE WHO AREN'T AFRAID TO LOOK FURTHER THAN THEY CAN SEE.

*Man's days are determined; you have decreed the number of his months and have set limits he cannot exceed.*

**JOB 14:5**

---

*My flesh and my heart fail; but God is the strength of my heart and my portion forever.*

**PSALM 73:25 NKJV**

---

*You saw me before I was born. Every day of my life was recorded in your book. Every moment was laid out before a single day had passed.*

**PSALM 139:16 NLT**

# LIFE LINES

D r. Jacobs had never been a patient in a hospital. He heard the symptoms—and the possible diagnosis. Neither was promising.

After years as a professor, scientist, and speaker in charge of many projects and students, it wasn't easy to not be in charge. But he trusted the One who was. Getting to know God over the years made talking to Him on this difficult day much easier. Those few moments with God helped take the fear out of the future and reminded him of the joy of today.

The illness Dr. Jacobs feared never materialized. But he did not regret his day of reckoning. For the first time, he knew his life was squarely in God's hands.

Have you given your life to God? He promises to treat it with the greatest of care.

THERE ARE THREE THINGS THAT ONLY GOD KNOWS: THE BEGINNING OF THINGS, THE CAUSE OF THINGS, AND THE END OF THINGS.

*My choice is you, God, first and only. And now I find I'm your choice!*

**PSALM 16:5 MSG**

---

*Remember this: Whoever sows sparingly will also reap sparingly, and whoever sows generously will also reap generously.*

**2 CORINTHIANS 9:6**

---

*"And do not fear those who kill the body but cannot kill the soul. But rather fear Him who is able to destroy both soul and body in hell. Are not two sparrows sold for a copper coin? And not one of them falls to the ground apart from your Father's will. But the very hairs of your head are all numbered. Do not fear therefore; you are of more value than many sparrows."*

**MATTHEW 10:28-31 NKJV**

# WHAT IS THAT LOUD BUZZING?

The day began with a buzzing alarm, a slap of the hand onto the snooze button, another buzzing, another slapping, another buzzing, and finally, a slow crawl out of bed. Before Tricia had invited her to church, Erica had always enjoyed sleeping in on Sunday mornings. No more.

But Tricia *was* a good friend, and there was something about this church that seemed to call to her almost as loudly as the alarm buzzer. Sometimes during the message, Erica would get a little sleepy—but not this morning. The pastor seemed to be talking directly to her. When he invited anyone seeking God to see him after the service, she was first in line.

Do you have a friend who needs to hear about the love of God? Do you have a friend who is hurting and could use some encouragement? Be a *real* friend; invite them to church where they can catch a glimpse of God.

> IT'S INCREDIBLY EXCITING TO CHOOSE TO FOLLOW GOD AND INFINITELY HUMBLING TO REALIZE GOD CHOSE YOU.

*"Put your mind on your life with God. The way to life—to God!—is vigorous and requires your total attention."*

**LUKE 13:24 MSG**

---

*He hath said, I will never leave thee, nor forsake thee.*

**HEBREWS 13:5 KJV**

---

*Let your heart therefore be loyal to the Lord our God, to walk in His statutes and keep His commandments, as at this day.*

**1 KINGS 8:61 NKJV**

# ROLE REVERSAL

Stephanie idolized her big sister, Sherrie. Sherrie was a straight-A student, scholarship magnet, and beauty queen. She was good at everything. Sherrie was Stephanie s inspiration.

But when Sherrie married and moved away, she pretty much gave up on God. "Don't have much time for that anymore, Steph," she said, during a rare Internet chat. Stephanie loved her big sister, but putting a relationship with God in the "if I have time" box didn't sit well with her. She prayed and caught a glimpse of God's undying love for Sherrie. So she kept praying.

Many years later, while visiting her younger sibling, Sherrie said, "I've messed up a ton in my life, but I want you to know I'm changing all that. In fact, I want to thank you."

"Thank me?" Stephanie said. "For what?"

"In high school and college I looked up to you, Sis. You took your relationship with God seriously. I didn't, and I paid the price. But you never gave up on me, and now I'm back."

> GOOD EXAMPLE HAS TWICE THE VALUE OF
> GOOD ADVICE.

*May the Lord of peace himself give you peace at all times and in every way.*

**2 THESSALONIANS 3:16**

---

*Trust in the Lord instead.*

**PSALM 37:3 TLB**

---

*I cried out, "I'm slipping!" and your unfailing love, O LORD, supported me. When doubts filled my mind, your comfort gave me renewed hope and cheer.*

**PSALM 94:18-19 NLT**

# LET IT FLY

Horseshoes wasn't a game Rory had ever longed to play. But when Granddad suggested he give it a go, he figured if he declined, cribbage would be next on the agenda. His grandfather began by putting several horseshoes in Rory's hand. "Weighty little buggers, aren't they?" Granddad said with a wink.

Rory watched his grandfather carefully pitch several horseshoes at the metal pin in the ground. Every shot made a satisfying "clank" as it reached its destination. His own attempts, however, showed considerably less success. Becoming discouraged, he asked his grandfather why he enjoyed this game so much. "I'll tell you why," Granddad said, with a sudden air of seriousness. "Every time I throw one of them horseshoes, I picture myself casting one of my problems on the Lord. By the time the game's finished, I always feel a lot better!"

Sometimes, casting your cares on the Lord works more like a boomerang than a horseshoe. The key is in the release.

---

CASTING OFF WHAT YOU DON'T NED MAKES IT EASIER TO HOLD ON TO WHAT YOU DO NEED.

*Hope deferred makes the heart sick,*
*but a longing fulfilled is a tree of life.*

**PROVERBS 13:12**

---

*"All that the Father gives me will come*
*to me; and him who comes to me I*
*will not cast out."*

**JOHN 6:37 RSV**

---

*"I am leaving you with a gift—peace*
*of mind and heart. And the peace I*
*give isn't like the peace that the world*
*gives. So don't be troubled or afraid."*

**JOHN 14:27 NLT**

# SWEET TREATS

Every year, it was a tough decision: turn on the porch light and welcome the kids in costume, or turn off the light and enjoy the bowl of Halloween candy herself. Once again, generosity (or was it guilt?) won out. Georgia turned on the light, and before she even made it down the hallway, the doorbell rang. When she opened the door, she was greeted by a frog and a fairy princess. "Trick or treat!" they yelled in unison.

Georgia placed a few goodies in each bag and thought, What a bizarre holiday! I'm glad that when I go to God, His promises are always good. He never threatens to trick me if I don't give Him something in return. She caught a glimpse of God's kindness that moment.

God doesn't hold a carrot in front of us, then pull it away. What He promises, He fulfills, even though we may not always see the results in a way we expect. Won't you open your heart and take hold of His promises for you?

> GOD'S PROMISES ARE, VIRTUALLY,
> OBLIGATIONS THAT HE IMPOSES ON HIMSELF.

*Don't indulge your ego at the expense of your soul.*

**1 PETER 2:11 MSG**

---

*Humble yourselves before the Lord and he will exalt you.*

**JAMES 4:10 RSV**

---

*Before destruction a man's heart is haughty, but humility goes before honor.*

**PROVERBS 18:12 RSV**

# LOOKING GOOD WHILE FALLING

James knew how to make an entrance. At his twentieth high school reunion, most of the whispers were about how good he looked. Among his professional colleagues, he was considered "most likely to marry a supermodel." Even his brothers revered him. Somewhere along the way all this adoration went to his head.

When it did, he began to distance himself from people who weren't "beautiful" enough. First to go were his brothers, both of whom worked blue-collar jobs. Many of his less successful business associates were next on the "cut" list. Even the "supermodels" he'd dated were deemed "not good enough" for someone as important as he was. When he messed up his shoulder and lost his professional sports career to injury, he took a job at a local high school coaching. As the blindfold of pride fell off in his darkest hour, he called out to God and found himself and the profession God had prepared for him.

At his twenty-fifth high school reunion, most of the hushed whispers were about how selfless and giving he'd become. A glimpse of God's love in his night of despair turned James to a passion for life — giving into the lives of others.

Giving into the lives of others gives the best rewards.

> **WHEN YOU GIVE OF YOURSELF—GIVE YOUR BEST.**

*If you stop your ears to the cries of the poor, your cries will go unheard, unanswered.*

**PROVERBS 21:13 MSG**

---

*Hereby perceive we the love of God, because he laid down his life for us: and we ought to lay down our lives for the brethren.*

**1 JOHN 3:16 KJV**

---

*When God's children are in need, be the one to help them out.*

**ROMANS 12:13 NLT**

# IN THE EYES

Helena had never seen such a sight before. The photograph of a young girl had grabbed her attention and wouldn't let go.

"Look at her," she said.

Kurt walked around behind Helena and looked over her shoulder. "I see an emaciated, hungry girl with sad eyes. But you know they just choose pictures like that so you'll send money."

"No, you're missing it. Look at her eyes."

Kurt pressed in closer, then said. "I don't know what I'm looking for."

"See the reflection in her eyes? I think you can see the photographer. "

"Okay, now I see it, so what's—hey, he looks—"

"Just like you?" she asked.

"Yeah—that's too weird." Kurt took the picture from Helena and studied it.

"This means something, Kurt."

"What, that we should send money?"

"No," she sighed, "what better way to make a difference than to be reflected in the eyes of a little child? I don't want to just send money, I want to send us."

---

**THEY SERVE GOD WELL WHO SERVE HIS CREATURES.**

*All my springs are in you.*

**PSALM 87:7 NKJV**

---

*Riches and honor are with me [Wisdom];
yea, durable riches and righteousness.*

**PROVERBS 8:18 KJV**

---

*A slack hand causes poverty, but the
hand of the diligent makes rich.*

**PROVERBS 10:4 RSV**

# JOY "LITE"

**D**oug admired his reflection in the hood of the sleekly waxed sports car. He had been heading across the lot to check out the used sedans, but right in his path was this bright red beauty. He checked the sticker price. It certainly wasn't a used sedan, but he could swing the payments, with a little proverbial belt tightening.

A moment's hesitation was all the salesman needed to explain how affordable this "fine piece of machinery" was. But as the salesman was speaking, one word echoed through Doug's head—*Why?* He had discussed this with God before. Different cars, different times, same discussion. Doug craved the admiration of others, and an eye-catching car was one way to get it. He mentally thanked God for the reminder, then asked the salesman to direct him to the used cars.

It's always good to listen for the real inner voice, reminding us that "joy" that can be bought is not real joy at all.

MATERIALISM IS ORGANIZED EMPTINESS OF THE SPIRIT.

*The work of righteousness shall be peace; and the effect of righteousness quietness and assurance for ever.*

**ISAIAH 32:17 KJV**

---

*"No weapon forged against you will prevail, and you will refute every tongue that accuses you."*

**ISAIAH 54:17**

---

*The angel of the Lord camps around those who fear God, and He saves them. Examine and see how good the Lord is. Happy is the person who trusts Him.*

**PSALM 34:7-8 NCV**

# INVISIBLE GIRDERS

During their third week, Frank observed that his Bible study group was like a crew of construction workers working on the foundation of their hearts. The next week, he wore a hard hat to the meeting. Everyone laughed at his joke. But it wasn't long before the hat became a symbol for the group. "When you're building a foundation, life can drop a lot of bricks on your head," he'd said.

One day Frank didn't show up. A few phone calls revealed the reason: he'd been injured and was in the hospital. After the group had filed into the small hospital room and prayed with him, they asked what happened. "Would you believe it? Bricks. Wouldn't have survived without this . . . ," he said, reaching under his bed.

Instead of a dented, scarred hard hat, he pulled out his Bible. Before our Bible study, I would have blamed God for this. No more, thanks to a good faith foundation—and a solid hat."

FAITH IS DELIBERATE CONFIDENCE IN THE CHARACTER OF GOD, WHOSE WAYS YOU CAN NOT UNDERSTAND AT THE TIME.

*"My people shall dwell in a peaceable habitation, and in sure dwellings, and in quiet resting places."*

**ISAIAH 32:18 KJV**

---

*To be carnally minded is death, but to be spiritually minded is life and peace.*

**ROMANS 8:6 NKJV**

---

*You will have confidence, because there is hope; you will be protected and take your rest in safety. You will lie down, and none will make you afraid.*

**JOB 11:18-19 RSV**

# DEEP REST

Sleepless nights — Vic had experienced hundreds of them. As a child, he didn't sleep because of severe allergies. He'd awake gasping for air and grasping for his inhaler. The teen years brought new sleep challenges because he was worried about his parents' divorce and his grandfather's terminal cancer. After college, his job stress doubled, and the nights became short once again. For a time, he tried sleeping pills. When he used them, he slept but woke up tired.

Out of desperation, Vic went looking for help. Counselors listened, but their solutions were temporary at best. It was a good friend who finally found the answer: a forced time of silence at the beginning and end of the day. Sleep began to come easier. Then Vic filled that time with prayer. Each day, he prayed for energy and peace. He got both. Now he sleeps deeply. Insomnia has been banished. But even beyond a good night's sleep, Vic has found something else: true rest.

> THAT WE AREN'T MUCH SICKER AND MUCH MADDER THAN WE ARE IS DUE EXCLUSIVELY TO THAT MOST BLESSED AND BLESSING OF ALL NATURAL GRACES — SLEEP.

*Let the peace of Christ keep you in tune with each other, in step with each other.*

**COLOSSIANS 3:15 MSG**

---

*Continue to love each other with true Christian love.*

**HEBREWS 13:1 NLT**

---

*Marriage should be honored by all.*

**HEBREWS 13:4**

# RHYTHM OF RELATIONSHIP

Gary wasn't about to miss an opportunity for another argument with Lynn. He wielded words like swords and verbally was quick on his feet. It might have been fun to watch the two battle had they been in a high school debate meet, but they were husband and wife.

"I'll tell you why you're wrong," was Gary's best opening move. He used it with such frequency, he almost didn't have to speak the words.

"Would you like to buy a clue?" was Lynn's favorite. No one ever won the battles. Both would walk away scarred, unfulfilled, and guarded, anticipating the next attack.

Peace didn't find its way into their lives until after church one Sunday. That's when their seven-year-old,

Tony, spoke up. "Mom—Dad, you're not supposed to fight. We're on the same team."

Something in that idea of a family team got to Gary and Lynn. That day, things began to change.

> KEEP YOUR EYES WIDE OPEN BEFORE
> MARRIAGE, HALF SHUT AFTERWARDS.

*God's plan for the world stands up, all his designs are made to last.*

**PSALM 33:11 MSG**

---

*The LORD is my strength and my shield; my heart trusted in him, and I am helped: therefore my heart greatly rejoiceth; and with my song will I praise him.*

**PSALM 28:7 KJV**

---

*"I also tell you this: If two of you agree down here on earth concerning anything you ask, My father in heaven will do it for you. For where two or three gather together because they are mine, I am there among them."*

**MATTHEW 18:19-20 NLT**

# SHORT LIST OF THE LONG-LASTING

L et's see — three coffee cups, one saucer, two plates, one serving dish, and a ceramic candle holder," Jennifer said, carefully picking up her coffee cup.

"All that in the last month?" Evelyn asked as she sipped her tea, more conscious than ever of the tiny crack in the cup handle.

"No — all that in the last week. I just seem to have a serious case of the dropsies." A loud crash interrupted Jennifer's thought. " — and a four-year-old," she finished.

"Things break. That's the way it is," Evelyn said as she set her cup gently onto the saucer.

"I sure wish my marriage hadn't broken," said Jennifer as she got up to investigate the crash.

"At least our friendship has stood the test of time," Evelyn called into the other room.

As she returned with a broken cup, Jennifer was smiling. "Yes, it has. And even when things are breaking all over, I know God's still in control." Another crash rang from the next room. "And I think He's telling me to buy plastic next time."

TO BE CAPABLE OF STEADY FRIENDSHIP AND LASTING LOVE ARE THE TWO GREATEST PROOFS, NOT ONLY OF GOODNESS OF HEART, BUT OF STRENGTH OF MIND.

*"Live out your God-created identity. Live generously and graciously toward others, the way God lives toward you."*

## MATTHEW 5:48 MSG

---

*The Lord will be your confidence and will keep your foot from being caught.*

## PROVERBS 3:26 RSV

---

*Do not conform any longer to the pattern of this world, but be transformed by the renewing of your mind. Then you will be able to test and approve what God's will is— his good, pleasing and perfect will.*

## ROMANS 12:2

"I can't believe he's the same person," Marcie said as she watched Jason walk to the snack table.

"Yeah, I know. Last year he was either obnoxiously drunk—or simply obnoxious," added Tina.

"I've got to know what happened," Marcie said. Then she walked over to refill her coffee cup and sidled up to Jason. "I hope I'm not being too nosy, but—you're not the same person I met last year at Jay's Super Bowl party."

He smiled and replied, "No, I'm not. Now I'm the real me. Back then, I was trying to be someone I'm not. I know it sounds corny when I say it, but I discovered the person God created me to be."

Marcie maintained a polite smile as she listened to his story; then she said, "Oh." It was all she knew to say. She excused herself and went back to Tina.

"He's some religious nut now," she offered.

Tina was intrigued. "Hey, learning to be comfortable in his own skin doesn't sound so nutty to me. Maybe I'll check into it myself. I know a few of the faculty around here who could use a shot of what he's got."

> RELIGION . . . IS IN ESSENCE THE RESPONSE
> OF CREATED PERSONALITIES TO THE
> CREATING PERSONALITY, GOD.

*With your very own hands you formed me; now breathe your wisdom over me so I can understand you.*

**PSALM 119:73 MSG**

---

*The depth of the riches of the wisdom and knowledge of God! How unsearchable his judgments, and his paths beyond tracing!*

**ROMANS 11:33**

---

*Happy is the person who finds wisdom and gains understanding. Wisdom is more precious than rubies; nothing you desire can compare with her. She offers you life in her right hand, and riches and honor in her left. She will guide you down delightful paths; all her ways are satisfying. Wisdom is a tree 6f life to those who embrace her; happy are those who hold her tightly.*

**PROVERBS 3:13, 15-18 NLT**

# INHALING THE BREATH OF GOD

Becoming a Christian had been a relatively easy decision for Gene. Though he felt no overwhelming change or any other emotional charge, he knew he'd joined God's family. Gaining wisdom and knowledge had always been important quests for him, so he was anxious to quickly learn all he could about God's wisdom.

"Lord, make me wise," he prayed. He dove into Bible study, reading every passage about wisdom he could find.

He wanted to know everything there was to know about wisdom—and he wanted to know it now. But Gene didn't sense any greater ability to reason, any hint of added discernment. In fact, it seemed as if God was silent. Weeks passed, and he felt no wiser.

Then one day he said in frustration, "God, I don't understand You—or anything much about this life." And he felt God draw near. That very day, Gene began to grow in wisdom.

KNOWLEDGE IS PROUD THAT HE HAS LEARNED SO MUCH; WISDOM IS HUMBLE THAT HE KNOWS NO MORE.

*Thanks be to God for his indescribable gift!*

## 2 CORINTHIANS 9:15

---

*Take heed that you do not do your charitable deeds before men, to be seen by them.*

## MATTHEW 6:1 NKJV

---

*Every man shall give as he is able, according to the blessing of the Lord your God which He has given you.*

## DEUTERONOMY 16:17 RSV

# OVERFLOWING

By the end of the day the boxes had been delivered, twenty-seven in all. Phil felt tired, but satisfied. He and Samantha had created a unique gift box for each of his students' families.

They boxed up food and gift certificates from local department stores for Serena's family. They gave Petey's family a basket of quick family meals for their busy family of seven. Terry's box contained a CD player and a gift certificate for a local music store for his and his mother's growing love of music.

"It's the best thing we've ever done," said Phil. "Since God has given us so much, it was obvious how we should spend that inheritance." They had also purchased dozens of movie ticket vouchers for the children as well. It was crazy, but Phil felt God's approval in it and a great deal of joy.

How about you? Is there something "crazy" God wants you to do?

WE ARE NEVER MORE LIKE GOD THAN WHEN WE GIVE.

*Commit your way to the Lord.*

**PSALM 37:5**

---

*"Be steadfast, immovable, always abounding in the work of the Lord, knowing that your labor is not in vain in the Lord."*

**1 CORINTHIANS 15:58 NKJV**

---

*"My grace is enough for you. When you are weak, my power is made perfect in you." So I am very happy to brag about my weaknesses. Then Christ's power can live in me.*

**2 CORINTHIANS 12:9 NCV**

# LIFE IN THE FAST LANE

Today Barbara's calendar looked more like a battle plan than a planner. Appointments spilled out of the box marked "Tuesday." Personal notes with red arrows filled every available margin. Barbara sighed and transferred her appointments and notes into her planning schedule. She needed two planning periods today. Ordinarily, she left breathing room in her day in case her students needed to speak with her, but sometimes things just snowballed. And today if one appointment ran long, or if Barbara got caught in traffic, that snowball was going to cause an avalanche.

So Barbara took one of her very valuable minutes to bow her head and commit her day to God. She realized that His plans for her might look a lot different than the list on this piece of paper, and she didn't want to miss His still, small voice amidst the hustle and bustle.

Each day, from the most extraordinary to the most ordinary, isn't really in your hands, but God's. This is true whether you commit it to Him or not.

SIMPLY WAIT UPON HIM. SO DOING, WE SHALL BE DIRECTED, SUPPLIED, PROTECTED, CORRECTED, AND REWARDED.

*Where the Spirit of the Lord is, there is freedom.*

**2 CORINTHIANS 3:17**

---

*Stand fast therefore in the liberty wherewith Christ hath made us free, and be not entangled again with the yoke of bondage.*

**GALATIANS 5:1 KJV**

---

*I shall walk at liberty, for I have sought thy precepts.*

**PSALM 119:45 RSV**

# FINALLY FREE

"**R**eligion is just a bunch of rules designed for people who can't live without them," Sheryl had always said. And Sheryl hated rules; perhaps that is why she got along better with the students she instructed than the faculty and staff. She liked purple hair, speaking her mind, and eating brownies for breakfast. She was convinced she had no use for God until one day when she found herself drawn to a "rule breaker" like herself.

He worked on Sundays when all the religious people said He shouldn't. He hung out with people of ill repute. He made grown-ups wait while He spent time with kids. And He wouldn't stay dead. But most radical of all, He didn't say, "Change, and then I'll love you." He said, "I love you the way you are." When Sheryl met Him, she found herself beginning to change—not her purple hair, but her heart.

Following God is not synonymous with following a set of religious rules. It's more like a heart makeover that sets you free to be who you really are.

---

**RELIGIOUS OFFERS RULES . . . GOD OFFERS RELATIONSHIP.**

*"Who of you by worrying can add a single hour to his life?"*

**MATTHEW 6:27**

---

*"Therefore do not worry, saying, 'What will we eat?' or 'What will we drink?' or 'What will we wear?' For after all these things the Gentiles seek. For your heavenly Father knows that you need all these things. But seek first the kingdom of God and His righteousness, and all these things shall be added to you. "*

**MATTHEW 6:31-33 NKJV**

---

*Cast all your anxieties on him, for he cares about you.*

**1 PETER 5:7 RSV**

# HURRIED WORRIES

Joyce was a champion worrier. She worried about her children so emphatically during their elementary school years that she would show up twice a week at school just to make sure they were okay. That, of course, was in addition to the three days she already volunteered in the classroom.

When her children went on to junior high and high school, she continued to keep close tabs on everything they did and everywhere they went. It was only a minor surprise, then, when she had a heart attack at forty-four years of age. When the news reached her now college-age children, they raced to the hospital to visit.

They barely entered the room when Mom spoke up through the oxygen mask, "You don't need to worry—I'm going to be fine."

In unison, they responded, "Look who's talking!" Joyce smiled. "God is here, and He told me things will be fine." And they were. She had begun to understand in this crisis that she didn't have to carry every concern herself.

How about you? Are you carrying things you should be giving to God?

WORRY NEVER ROBS TOMORROW OF ITS SORROW; IT ONLY SAPS TODAY OF ITS STRENGTH.

*Who despises the day of small things?*

**ZECHARIAH 4:10**

---

*"You did well. You are a good and loyal servant. Because you were loyal with small things, I will let you care for much greater things."*

**MATTHEW 25:23 NCV**

---

*Let God bless all who fear God—bless the small, bless the great.*

**PSALM 115:13 MSG**

# NOT INSIGNIFICANT

Nate had tinkered with the computer for three hours, trying without success to find out why it wouldn't boot up. He had replaced the video card, the CPU, the power supply, and even the sound card, but nothing seemed to work. He was dreading the thought of having to take the beast to the repair shop. That computer was his livelihood. He couldn't give it up for even a day, let alone the week it would sit in the repair shop.

As he was about to give up, he stopped and prayed, "God, I probably should have asked You at the beginning of this, but I could really use Your insight." He sat quietly for some moments. Then he noticed a tiny wire hanging free inside the case. Upon careful inspection, he determined it connected the case's power button to the motherboard. "Aha! Found you!" he exclaimed. Sure enough, once the tiny wire was plugged in, the computer started up without a hitch.

Things at work got you puzzled? Ask God to help. He is good at solving puzzles.

SOMETIMES THE SMALLEST THINGS CAN HAVE THE GREATEST POWER.

*I will remove from them their heart of stone and give them a heart of flesh.*

**EZEKIEL 11:19**

---

*We should continue following the truth we already have. Brothers and sisters, all of you should try to follow my example and to copy those who live the way we showed you.*

**PHILIPPIANS 3:16-17 NCV**

---

*Let no one despise your youth, but be an example to the believers in word, in conduct, in love, in spirit, in faith, in purity.*

**1 TIMOTHY 4:12 NKJV**

# STONE COLD

Three years — that's how long Jan had been praying for Mary to explore a relationship with God. Jan hadn't been obnoxious. In fact, it wasn't until three months into their friendship that she had even mentioned she went to church.

Mary simply said, "Good for you."

In time, they came to a mutual understanding about their beliefs. Each said, "I'm not going to hide what I believe, but I won't force my beliefs down your throat." Perhaps because of this honest approach, they developed a strong bond. When Jan's mother passed away, Mary and some other teachers substituted for her classes while Jan and her husband went to Florida for the funeral. When Mary had a heart attack, Jan visited often and took care of her three dogs.

One day, however, Jan saw the first crack in Mary's heart. "This God of yours is tapping on my heart," she said. Jan couldn't restrain her broad smile.

Do your actions draw others to God?

> **A THOUSAND WORDS WILL NOT LEAVE AS DEEP AN IMPRESSION AS ONE DEED.**

*I do not understand my own actions. For I do not do what I want, but I do the very thing I hate.*

**ROMANS 7:15 RSV**

---

*"By your words you will be justified, and by your words you will be condemned."*

**MATTHEW 12:37 NKJV**

---

*Those who are careful about what they say keep themselves out of trouble.*

**PROVERBS 21:23 NCV**

# BACKING INTO TROUBLE

"Driver's license and registration," the policeman ordered. "Out of the wallet." As Paul reached into his wallet, he wondered if all officers had such eloquent speaking ability. Of course, he wasn't one to talk. His mouth had gotten him into trouble countless times.

Paul wasn't a mean-spirited person. Most of the time, students and faculty alike appreciated his dry wit. But sometimes his wit would take the form of a dragon, and his words would scorch all in their path. He never intended to hurt anyone, but the fallout was devastating. It. even cost him his marriage.

Some days Paul felt as if all he did was apologize. "I'm sorry, Officer," he said, snapping back to the moment. "I didn't see that car when I was backing up."

Tearing off the ticket, the officer spoke three words, "Look next time."

Paul knew instantly this was God's wise advice for all of his life, and he said, "I will, Officer."

Think about ways you can be careful about your words.

---

**WORDS ARE LIKE LOADED PISTOLS.**

*If you do not stand firm in your faith, you will not stand at all.*

**ISAIAH 7:9**

---

*If someone mistreats you because you are a Christian, don't curse him; pray that God will bless him.*

**ROMANS 12:14 TLB**

---

*Take a firm stand against him, and be strong in your faith.*

**1 PETER 5:9 NLT**

# WAR OF WORDS

"**A**nyone who believes in a God who communicates on a personal level with mere mortals has got to be an idiot," Hugh announced authoritatively. Those who were gathered around in the teacher's lounge didn't say a word. Everyone knew that Hugh wasn't one to take opposition lightly.

On the outside, Monica was peacefully munching on a bag of potato chips, but inside, she felt a war erupting. Hugh's words went against everything she believed to be true, but she didn't know what to do. Should she speak up, engage Hugh in a conversation, or just hold her tongue and add him to her prayer list?

Passing through the lounge, but aware of their conversation, the assistant principal piped up, "For one who opposes religion so much, you certainly give it place in your life and conversation. Perhaps you should think about that. Maybe God's trying to communicate with you. Listen and see what He says."

Monica pondered those words, *The "Hughs" of the world want nothing more than to hear that what they believe is untrue — that they really can know a personal God who cares for them individually.* The vice principal's words were as if God had popped in and shared a glimpse of His heart for Hugh.

---

TRUTH IS INCONTROVERTIBLE. PANIC MAY RESENT IT; IGNORANCE MAY DERIDE IT; MALICE MAY DISTORT IT; BUT THERE IT IS.

---

*I have set before you life and death, blessings and curses. Now choose life.*

**DEUTERONOMY 30:19**

---

*Your sins affect only people like yourself, and your good deeds affect only other people.*

**JOB 35:8 NLT**

---

*When I sit in the darkness, the Lord shall be a light unto me.*

**MICAH 7:8 KJV**

# CHAIN REACTION

**M**aybe it was not enough hot water to finish his shower that morning. Maybe it was a restless night's sleep. Maybe it was the thought of all the tests he would have to grade this weekend. Whatever it was, Jeremy was in a bad mood. And everyone who crossed his path would know it.

When he got up, he kicked the dog, who chased the cat, who tormented the rat, and on and on. You know the story. But picture what Jeremy passed on to the people he connected with that day—his wife and kids, his students and coworkers, the waitress at the coffee shop, and the phone solicitor who called at dinnertime.

Suddenly Jeremy saw a picture of his attitude that day. At his wife's suggestion, he took a moment to reconnect with God and acknowledge his lack of patience and kindness for those around him. Tonight he could break the cycle. Tomorrow would be a better day. He could feel God's assurance on that.

Life isn't lived in a vacuum. Your actions affect everyone around you. Choose to be a positive influence in other people's lives each day.

> YOU CANNOT ADD TO THE PEACE AND GOOD WILL OF THE WORLD IF YOU FAIL TO CREATE AN ATMOSPHERE OF HARMONY AND LOVE RIGHT WHERE YOU LIVE AND WORK.

*"Not by might nor by power, but by my Spirit."*

**ZECHARIAH 4:6**

---

*The Lord upholds all who fall, and raises up all who are bowed down.*

**PSALM 145:14 NKJV**

---

*Thanks be to God, who always leads us in victory through Christ.*

**2 CORINTHIANS 2:14 NCV**

# GROWING STRONG

The fall day had a slight nip in the air, but the warmth of the sun overpowered it. It was the perfect day for a field trip through the canyon. After an hour or so, Rebecca told her students she'd catch up with them. She wanted to spend a few moments alone with God, enjoying the beauty that surrounded her. As she took a drink out of her canteen, her eyes caught sight of an evergreen tree growing out of the side of the sheer cliff wall.

*I can't even get herbs to grow in pots on my protected window sill,* she thought in amazement. *Somehow that seed fell into enough soil to thrive. I guess God just wanted it there.* Rebecca reflected on how God had the same plan for her life. Unwanted as a child, she was adopted into a great family. Now she couldn't imagine growing up anywhere else. Indeed, God grows great lives under less-than-ideal circumstances.

BEFORE GOD CREATED THE UNIVERSE, HE
ALREADY HAD YOU IN MIND.

*Everyone should be quick to listen, slow to speak and slow to become angry.*

**JAMES 1:19**

---

*Patient people have great understanding, but people with quick tempers show their foolishness.*

**PROVERBS 14:29 NCV**

---

*Scoffers set a city aflame, but wise men turn away wrath.*

**PROVERBS 29:8 NKJV**

# SHORT FUSE

A muddy trail led upstairs, right to Brittany's room. Sonya headed up to confront her daughter. As usual, she was on the phone; her room was a disaster, including the pile of clothes Sonya had just washed that morning. Sonya grabbed the phone out of her hand before her daughter could even voice her good-byes. "I didn't do it! It's not my fault!" was Brittany's angry retort to her mother's insistence that she clean the carpet this minute.

"How stupid do you think I am?" Sonya snapped back. "You left a trail!" Sonya slammed the door on her way out. Though she was fuming, she could hear God whisper how out of control she was. In her anger, she denied any wrongdoing, accusing Brittany of being the real culprit. She heard herself saying, "It's not my fault!" but stopped short when she heard God's reply: *You left a trail.*

Even when we don't tell ourselves the truth, God will.

CONSCIENCE IS GOD'S PRESENCE IN MAN.

*"If you make yourselves at home with me and my words are at home in you, you can be sure that whatever you ask will be listened to and acted upon."*

**JOHN 15:7 MSG**

---

*But you, beloved, building yourselves up on your most holy faith, praying in the Holy Spirit, keep yourselves in the love of God, looking for the mercy of our Lord Jesus Christ unto eternal life.*

**JUDE 1:20-21 NKJV**

---

*The prayer of the righteous man has great power in its effects.*

**JAMES 5:16 RSV**

# IS ANYBODY LISTENING?

Julia opened the door to the art room supply closet and sighed. Not that she really expected anyone would have cleaned it while she was at a state convention, but she had asked the kids to keep it straight. Three times. She kicked at a pile of dirty smocks, then shut the door again. It was better not to look.

Some days, Julia felt that trying to communicate with her students was like talking to her houseplants—a total waste of time. "If just once someone would actually listen to me!" she grumbled. *I will*, she felt God reply.

Imagine if you had something to say only once to be heard. Now imagine not only being heard but also understood and responded to. God is not only listening, but He's also ready to act when you speak to Him. He's not your personal genie in a bottle, ready to fulfill your every wish, but He works through your prayers to bring about the fulfillment of His purposes in your life. How can you make yourself more "at home" with Him?

---

PRAYER IS THE KEY OF HEAVEN; FAITH IS THE
HAND THAT TURNS IT.

---

*There is no fear in love, but perfect love casts out fear.*

**1 JOHN 4:18 RSV**

---

*For I the LORD thy God will hold thy right hand, saying unto thee, Fear not; I will help thee.*

**ISAIAH 41:13 KJV**

---

*Those who listen to me will live in safety and be at peace, without fear of injury.*

**PROVERBS 1:33 NCV**

# NO FEAR

As a twelve-year-old, John used to lie awake listening to the sounds of the night. When his parents hosted visitors for the evening, he would strain to hear their conversations and fall asleep easily to the familiar rhythm of voices. But when there were no voices, he could not sleep. Even as an adult, the foreign creaks and groans that littered the night opened his eyes wide in fear. Even the somewhat familiar sound of the furnace seemed suddenly menacing in the dark.

In the last few years, however, John had found God and the power of prayer. He prayed during those nights — that he might fall asleep and that the sounds would go away. In those prayers, he pictured a loving God — a God who would not want him to feel afraid. He learned that God's love was bigger than fear, and sleep soon became his companion in the dark.

Don't let fear rob you of your peace. Entrust yourself to God.

GOD INCARNATE IS THE END OF FEAR; AND THE HEART THAT REALIZES THAT HE IS IN THE MIDST . . . WILL BE QUIET IN THE MIDST OF ALARM.

# ACKNOWLEDGEMENTS

(14) Joseph D. Blinco, (16) W. D. Gough, (22) Mary Bryant, (26) Oliver Wendell Holmes, (28) Bertha Munro, (30) Francis Quarles, (32) Richard Clarke Cabot, (Thomas La Mance), (44) Corrie ten Boom, (46) Francis Thompson, (48,74) Francis de Sales, (50) Augustine of Hippo, (52) Jewish Proverb, (54) Honore De Balzac, (56) Albert Benjamin Simpson, (58) John Donne, (62) G. S. Lewis, (64) Elbert Green Hubbard, (66,178) A. W. Tozer, (68) Joni Eareckson Tada, (70) Oswald Chambers, (82) Bill Gothard, (88) Erwin W. Lutzer, (90) William Barclay, (92) Cardinal John Henry Newman, (94) Alfred North Whitehead, (96) Oswald Chambers, (98) Charles Haddon Spurgeon, (loo) Robert Harold Schuller, (102) A. W. Tozer, (104) Agnes Maude Royden, (108) Billy Graham, (no) Robert Cecil, (ll2, 206) F. B. Meyer, (116) Adam Clarke, (120) Alexander MacLaren, (128) Meister Eckhart, (146) Dwight L. Moody, (154) Welsh Proverb, (162) Friedrich Wilhelm Krummacher, (167) Caroline Sheridan Norton, (168) Franz Werfel, (1.70, 172) Aldous Huxley, (174) Benjamin Franklin, (176) William Hazlitt, (180) William Cowper, (182) Charles R. Swindoll, (184) Vance Havner, (188) Archibald Joseph Cronin, (192) Henrik Ibsen, (194) Jean Paul Sartre, (196) Sir Winston Churchill, (198) Thomas Dreier, (200) Edwin W. Lutzer, (202) Emanuel Swedenborg.

Additional copies of this book and other titles from
Honor Books are available from your local bookstore.

*Glimpses of an Invisible God*

*Glimpses of an Invisible God - for Women*

*Glimpses of an Invisible God - for Mothers*

*Glimpses of an Invisible God - for Teens*